IN THE BELLY OF THE BEAR

IN THE BELLY OF THE BEAR

An FBI Journey behind the New Iron Curtain

JEFFREY IVERSON

SPECIAL AGENT OF THE
FEDERAL BUREAU OF INVESTIGATION (RETIRED)

ROWMAN & LITTLEFIELD
Lanham • Boulder • New York • London

Published by Rowman & Littlefield
An imprint of The Rowman & Littlefield Publishing Group, Inc.
4501 Forbes Boulevard, Suite 200, Lanham, Maryland 20706
www.rowman.com

86-90 Paul Street, London EC2A 4NE

British Library Cataloguing in Publication Information Available

Library of Congress Cataloging-in-Publication Data
Names: Iverson, Jeffrey, author.
  Title: In the belly of the bear : an FBI journey behind the new iron
    curtain / Jeffrey Iverson, Special Agent of the Federal Bureau of
    Investigation (Retired).
  Description: Lanham : Rowman & Littlefield, [2024] | Includes
    bibliographical references and index. | Summary: "Former FBI agent
    Jeffery Iverson chronicles the collaboration between the FBI and Russian
    authorities in the decades following the fall of the Soviet Union. Part
    cultural history, part international thriller, Iverson details
    successful criminal and terrorism investigations between the FBI and
    former Soviet authorities before the rise of Putin"-- Provided by
    publisher.
  Identifiers: LCCN 2023041432 (print) | LCCN 2023041433 (ebook) | ISBN
    9781538189139 (cloth) | ISBN 9781538189146 (ebook)
  Subjects: LCSH: United States. Federal Bureau of Investigation--History. |
    United States--Foreign relations--Soviet Union. | United States--Foreign
    relations--Russia.
  Classification: LCC HV8144.F43 I84 2024 (print) | LCC HV8144.F43 (ebook)
    | DDC 363.250973--dc23/eng/20230927
  LC record available at https://lccn.loc.gov/2023041432
  LC ebook record available at https://lccn.loc.gov/2023041433

To Les McNulty and his affable and able New York partner, FBI agents who were showing the rest of us how to do this while we were still trying to figure out what hit us.

The opinions expressed in this book are those of the author, not of the FBI.

Contents

CONTENTS

CHAPTER 1

Stepping Out of Our Shelters

WHAT MAKES A MAN (OR WOMAN) LEAVE HIS COMFORTABLE CALIFOR-
nia bubble for countries halfway around the world, where he knows no
one and has little understanding of the language, culture, or religion?
What makes him go from one of the most beautiful cities on the planet
to regions struggling to overcome decades of Soviet decay? *What was I
thinking?* That was the question I would ask myself many times starting
in the late 1990s—a knee-jerk reaction to novel challenges I would face
in Russia and remote corners of the former Soviet Union, where the rules
of the road were turned on their head, and streets were paved with chaos,
corruption, and political repression. These were unfamiliar worlds, where
a cultural disregard for personal safety was an occupational hazard, and
isolation paradoxically went hand in hand with unwelcome intrusions
into one's privacy. But leave my comfortable bubble I did, and despite the
challenges, I never looked back.

I grew up in the outskirts of Chicago during a turbulent period in the
Windy City's history. From the 1960s through the mid-1980s, Chicago
was the setting for headline-grabbing events that would one day help me
appreciate how dissent, power politics, and official corruption impacted
life in both the former Soviet Union and its offspring, the Russian Federation. I was first exposed to those events during the 1968 Democratic
National Convention, where I was one voice among thousands of young
protesters—some unhinged, many simply idealistic, but all committed
to giving peace a chance. Two years later, I marched in peaceful demonstrations prompted by the National Guard's fatal shooting of four Kent

State students, where we voiced our dissent in an atmosphere charged with the bumper sticker sentiment: "America—Love it or leave it." In 1974, as I was beginning my graduate studies in social work, my journey took a right turn that coincided with my after-school role as an assistant precinct captain for Richard J. Daley's legendary political machine; a supplement to my formal education that provided me a good look at how those in power stayed in power. And for six years prior to being sworn in as an FBI agent, I was a social worker with a front-row seat in Chicago's criminal courts, where judges were dropping like flies on federal corruption charges.[1]

But like every kid in my generation, I grew up watching another side of history unfold. Although I was far too young to understand the politics, I wasn't too young to sense something ominous about tanks rolling into the streets of faraway cities as the Iron Curtain descended on Eastern Europe. I was part of a generation that grew up under the dark cloud of the Cold War, with black-and-white images of the Berlin Wall, the frantic race to build bigger and better bombs, and the Cuban Missile Crisis, when the world stood one momentary miscalculation away from a catastrophic meltdown. As small children, these were indelible images we understood on a gut level. They were lasting imprints on impressionable young minds, a steady drumbeat of hazy gray, thermonuclear nightmares, fed by the slogan "Better dead than Red" and measured both in megatons of mushrooming fireballs and countdowns on a doomsday clock. In short, I was a scared kid. And what was the source of my fears? The hammer and sickle. The godless Communists. The Russian Bear.

In 2003, as I mulled over the decision to leave California behind me, one window into my thinking was an interest in all things Russian, a by-product of the criminal threat that followed the breakup of the Soviet Union in 1991. By the mid-1990s, that seismic shift in global dynamics had set off waves of cascading changes, some of which galvanized the FBI into forming Russian organized crime squads across the United States. What was our mission? To fend off criminal groups whose cross-border tentacles were growing ever more muscular, bolstered by globalization and a shrinking world. To head off that threat, agents with backgrounds in organized crime were sent to former Soviet Bloc countries to promote

FBI leadership in this emerging field. Our task was to rally teams of foreign police investigators and train former Soviet Bloc police managers on strategies to take down notorious Russian criminals and dismantle their ever-expanding enterprises. Much of our training took place at the International Law Enforcement Academy in Budapest, where paved-over potholes in downtown streets were battle scars left by recent organized crime car bombings, and bullet holes in downtown buildings were a grim reminder of the heyday of the KGB and Hungary's ill-fated uprising against Soviet domination in 1956. But by the late 1990s, the Soviet Union's ominous shadow over Eastern Europe had faded as the world collectively scratched its head, trying to figure out what came next. Was I bored? Certainly not. Was I burnt out? Maybe a little. But above all, the decision to venture out was in keeping with a series of adventures that were part and parcel of the organization I loved . . . warts and all.

What follows is my take on an intriguing former Soviet world as seen by an FBI agent with a ringside seat, colored by the memories of that Cold War kid. It is based on the last half of my twenty-two-year career, during which consequential events in that region were my exclusive focus. That includes a brief window in time, years after the fall of the Berlin Wall, when the lingering shadow of that once-frightened child crawled out of his shelter long enough to experience a beautiful and profoundly human side of the "other"—a time when it seemed plausible that the US and Russia might set aside their decades-long, danger-laden animosity. But a darker side of this story is the steep ascent of Soviet thinking that reemerged in the early 2000s, which later overlapped with America's descent into homegrown assaults on the democratic values, institutions, and alliances that were once the tip of the spear in our victory over Ronald Reagan's "Evil Empire." This has called into question not only our once-undisputed status as victors in the Cold War but also the direction in which our cherished democracy is now headed.

CHAPTER 2

Into the Belly of the Bear

THERE ARE SEVERAL THEORIES AS TO HOW BEARS CAME TO SYMBOLIZE Russia. Russia's official symbol is the double-headed eagle, but the bear appears to have been imposed on Russia by outsiders, including nineteenth-century political cartoonists in Great Britain and the US. In an article from the publication *Russia Beyond*, the author sets out various theories as to how the symbol evolved. Among them is Tsar Ivan the Terrible's use of bears as a means of execution. Another theory involves Russia's history of training bears to perform in circuses. Regardless of its origin, in the words of the author, during the Cold War, "the bear became a metaphor for the cruel, bloodthirsty policies of the USSR."[1] Many of us who grew up during the Cold War can relate to that conclusion, if only in our fear-fueled imaginations.

Several factors drew me to the former Soviet Union. Among my peers, we used the lighthearted-yet-somewhat-unflattering term "hot spotter" to describe an agent who maneuvers his or her way into the action. For me and many of my peers, the action was overseas, where recent developments were having a powerful impact on the work of the FBI. So in 2003, as we were digging out of our emotional 9/11 rubble, the former Central Asian republics drew my attention, given their Soviet roots and their proximity to the same brand of terrorism that took down the Twin Towers. Moscow was an even bigger draw, given its position on the front lines of the criminal threat fueled by the breakup of the Soviet Union. But in hindsight, it is clear that I had deeper, more personal reasons for my preoccupation with the former Soviet Union, some having to do with the fear of the "other" that I grew up with. Regardless of the reasons, one thing was certain: the FBI offered the perfect platform from which to get in the game, witness a slice of history, and draw me out of my Cold War shelter.

Amid these developments I was supervising San Francisco's Russian Organized Crime squad, a small team of dedicated, young agents and support professionals, each of whom brought their share of energy and investigative muscle to the table. The heart of my squad included a former CIA Soviet analyst, two attorneys, a PhD in psychology, a CPA, an ex-cop, a geologist, a San Francisco-born Russian linguist, and this former social worker. Our mission was to target a new group of criminals penetrating the FBI's radar—the by-product of the drastic changes that were taking place in what was, by then, the "former" Soviet Union. Among those changes was the newfound freedom of former Soviet citizens to invest in, do business with, and immigrate to the US.[2]

Soon after the collapse of the Soviet Union, a fresh wave of Russian-speaking immigrants began arriving in the United States. Many gravitated to larger cities such as New York and San Francisco, where their Russian-speaking ancestors had settled before and after the Bolshevik Revolution. Those early arrivals were followed, starting in the 1970s, by a second wave of Soviets—Jewish émigrés—who began settling in the US after years of international pressure on Soviet authorities to allow Jewish citizens to leave the Soviet Union.

Among the most recent post-Soviet group were those who'd made a clean break with their past to build a new life in a once-forbidden American world: to study, advance their careers, raise families, and/or establish legitimate businesses. Among them were those who left the former Soviet Union to escape the violence and economic uncertainty that defined life in the 1990s—a chaotic atmosphere (especially in Russia) where, as in Soviet times, government institutions were paralyzed by corruption and tangled bureaucracies. Chief among the former Soviet Union's most feared institutions was the KGB, a shadowy organization that Russian-speaking immigrants often equated with the FBI. That misperception complicated the FBI's work, given an inherent mistrust of government that had tainted former Soviets' perception of the US judicial system, leaving many to believe they had little choice but to submit to a shadow system of justice controlled by criminally connected members within their community.

Those with a shady past included garden-variety criminals who preyed on fellow Soviet immigrants through extortion, kidnapping, and violence. Others preyed on their own through fraudulent get-rich-quick schemes that appealed to recent immigrants' easy-money fantasies and their mistrust of traditional avenues of investment. And yet others were nonviolent criminals who had honed their skills by exploiting cracks in the Soviet economic structure. Among the latter were those who traded on the Soviet black market, a dangerous world where corruption was rampant and organized crime ruled. In that world traffickers supplied fellow Soviets with contraband or items in short supply, including anything from the West: clothing, food, luxury items, and a variety of everyday needs. But even for the many who steered clear of violating Soviet law, finding cracks in the Soviet system had simply been a survival tool, born of a culture in which, for the average citizen, access to everyday needs was a challenge, and pulling oneself up by the bootstraps was little more than a distant capitalist concept. The end result? Those who were skilled at beating the Soviet system found the US system easy prey—a twist on America's reputation as the land of opportunity.[3] Cases in point:

International Money laundering became a significant problem after the collapse of the Soviet Union, due, in part, to a new class of wealthy former Soviets who emerged as Russia underwent its transformation from communism to capitalism. Within the Russian community, those individuals were sometimes sarcastically referred to as "Novie Russkie" (New Russians), a play on their success at exploiting Russia's new version of private enterprise that was once strictly forbidden under communism. Among them were those who found the US a safe place to legitimately invest and grow their newfound wealth. Less scrupulous New Russians found the US the preferred setting to launder millions of dollars stolen from their newly formed governments—wealth that was often generated through scams that tapped into the former Soviet Union's vast natural resources. In many cases those scams were enabled by corrupt Russian politicians and, in some cases, by rogue American bank employees and businessmen who, having sensed an opportunity in the free-for-all underway, were credibly accused of collectively laundering billions of dollars on behalf of their Russian clients.[4]

On a far smaller scale, schemes to disguise the nature of Russian-based financial transactions and/or to hide assets from Russian authorities included the creation of bogus US businesses set up by Russians with the assistance of US-based confederates. Despite their façade of legitimacy, those "businesses" consisted of little more than a company name and a four-by-twelve-inch mailbox in a roomful of identical "offices," each posing as a legitimate business address with a "suite" number that corresponded to the number on the mailbox. In those early days, Russia-based owners of these US-based businesses were sometimes able to remotely open US bank accounts with little more than a faxed photocopy of a Russian passport—clearly, a breach of the "know your customer" due diligence banking rule.

Medicare fraud centered on kickback schemes that were unique in their design, scope, and simplicity. In some large cities, those schemes were built around close-knit groups of former Soviet doctors who exploited their ability to refer their elderly Russian-speaking patients for medically unnecessary blood tests, medical equipment, and prescription medication. Those expensive services were typically satisfied by locally based blood labs, medical equipment providers, and pharmacies run by former Soviets. Each player got their share of the Medicare pie at US government expense, with kickbacks to the organizers of the scheme.

Staged auto accidents were another uniquely Russian specialty that emerged in large cities across the US, a form of insurance fraud in which vehicle owners preplanned accidents. The "injured" then made fraudulent insurance claims that potentially benefitted both parties to the accident, as well as Russian-owned repair shops, the lawyers who sued the insurance companies to cover injuries, and the doctors who could be counted on to verify the "severity" of those injuries. All of this resulted in huge losses for insurance companies.

Fugitives from Russia and other former Soviet republics, including members of violent organized criminal groups, were drawn to the Bay Area, where, if they kept a low profile, they could seamlessly blend into

San Francisco's Russian-speaking community. The Bay Area was their hole-in-the-wall where they could whitewash their sordid past in a live-and-let-live culture known for its mistrust of and hostility toward law enforcement. And since there was no extradition treaty between the US and Russia, the FBI rarely had a legal basis on which to arrest and/or deport these individuals based on Russian criminal charges alone, despite having a good sense of their violent history.

In short, while the West was celebrating its Cold War victory, the former Soviet Union was in a state of chaos as its citizens struggled to regain their footing and digest the new rules governing their world. Of concern to the FBI were the criminal groups that were exploiting that confusion, battling for a share of the loot that was up for grabs amid political and economic turmoil. Some members of those groups fled to the West to hide assets stolen from their countries' governments. Others came to the US to dodge criminal charges in their home countries. Among the latter were those who violently preyed on fellow former Soviets living in the US. And yet others, skilled at beating the Soviet economic system, applied that expertise in the US, where they took advantage of vulnerabilities in government programs, businesses, and their fellow immigrants' predilection for off-the-books investments, leaving those novice investors little recourse upon discovering they had been scammed. And how did the FBI respond to this new brand of fallout blowing in from the East? Agents new to the world of Russian organized crime had to brush up on their understanding of Russian culture and the mechanics behind Russia's transformation from communism to capitalism.[5]

"They pretend to pay us, and we pretend to work" (Они делают вид, что платят, мы делаем вид, что работаем) is a popular Russian saying that captures the fallacies built into the workers' paradise theory of communism—an ideology that dominated the economic, political, work, family, and social life of all Russians starting in October 1917.[6] With the founding of the Soviet Union in 1922 and with various iterations of the KGB as its ironfisted enforcer, the Communist Party remained the Soviet Union's sole authorized political party until 1990, when authorities officially recognized the Liberal Democratic Party of the Soviet Union, a collaboration between the Communist Party and the KGB. At its peak in the mid-1980s, the Communist Party of the Soviet Union boasted approximately nineteen million members, many of whom held leadership positions in government, factories, collective farms, the media, military, and universities, where they controlled the levers of power.

Unlike a US citizen's simple decision to identify as a member of a political party, membership in the Communist Party of the Soviet Union entailed completing rites of passage that began in childhood. Aspiring members had to be accepted into the party and carefully screened prior to approval. They typically needed support from well-established party members, who vouched for their loyalty and their adherence to party principles. Once accepted, party members found membership privileges might include choice apartments, preferred access to respected universities for their children, more desirable dachas (cottages in the country), and access to goods normally unavailable to ordinary citizens. In some cases party members were granted exit visas—travel privileges unavailable to ordinary citizens, allowing them limited travel outside the Soviet Union. Membership was also considered a means of achieving upward mobility, an important stepping-stone toward management positions gained through access to specialized training and favorable evaluations by fellow Communists.[7]

In many ways communism's workers' paradise was built on smoke and mirrors. It was a world in which the state owned everything: land, farms, city apartments, factories, the means of production, natural resources, and mass media outlets, where private ownership had little meaning. In this nationalized, top-down, command economy, artificial production and price controls stood in for the laws of supply and demand. Incentives for ordinary citizens to work hard were minimal, but choosing not to work was not an option, exposing one to charges of *social parasitism*. It was a system in which artificially inflated agricultural and manufacturing statistics might reflect well on party bosses but simultaneously camouflage the faltering production of essential commodities. These and other factors led to long lines to purchase the most basic daily needs. Those shortages also contributed to the formation of an underground economy in which black marketeers, in partnership with corrupt government officials, sold contraband from the West and commodities skimmed from Soviet factories and collective farms to Soviet citizens. On the black market, goods and services were often traded using illegal currencies, especially the US dollar, all of which resulted in a world where merchants dodged (or paid off) police officials and other government bureaucrats. In defiance of Soviet law, the black market operated according to unwritten rules enforced by organized crime bosses known as "Vory v zakone" (thieves in law).

Communist control of the levers of power would have implications down the road, placing those who once held leadership positions in government, factories, farms, and industry in a position of advantage as the Soviet Union collapsed. Those advantages began to play out after August 1991, when a group of die-hard Soviet loyalists led by the head of the KGB and other high-ranking Soviet officials staged what would become a failed coup against Soviet leader Mikhail Gorbachev, whose reform policies—glasnost (open government) and perestroika (restructuring)—were perceived by leaders of the coup as having gone too far. As the coup headed toward collapse, Boris Yeltsin became a symbol of Russia's emerging break from communism as he bravely stood atop a tank at the Russian Parliament in defiance of the coup. In a speech that day, Yeltsin appealed to the "citizens of Russia," notably failing to address his audience as "citizens of the Soviet Union."[8] In a series of rapidly developing events following the coup, Gorbachev effectively banned the Communist Party and disbanded the KGB. He resigned from office on December 25, 1991, and within days, the Soviet Union collapsed. Left in its wake were fifteen sovereign states, one of which would become the Russian Federation that Yeltsin had been leading since the previous July, following his inauguration to the position of president of the Russian Soviet Federative Socialist Republic. Soon after those momentous developments, Boris Yeltsin, Russia's first popularly elected leader, took possession of Russia's nuclear codes and moved into his new home in the Kremlin.

As president of the Russian Federation, Yeltsin shouldered the monumental task of *privatization*—the chaotic process of transferring state-owned assets to private ownership and management that was the hallmark of Russia's transition from communism to capitalism. Those assets included Russia's crown jewels—factories, farms, land, buildings, oil, gas, timber, aluminum, nickel, minerals, and precious metals (and diamonds) that, under communism, were owned by the Soviet state. In this effort Yeltsin had the overall approval and limited (some say grossly inadequate) support of the West. But the new Russian Federation under Yeltsin grew into a state of chaos as he appointed and fired several cabinets. While he was drinking, clowning, and struggling to lead, Russia's state-owned assets were being picked clean by a combustible mix of competing centers of power—future oligarchs, heads of organized crime groups, and former Soviet government officials.

In theory, the 1991 collapse of the Soviet Union opened new economic opportunities for citizens, who were suddenly allowed to accumulate wealth, assume ownership of their apartments, establish businesses, and travel to foreign countries. But those who once held positions of power in the Soviet system and/or those with the right connections had a leg up, given their proximity to the vast assets under the control of the state and their role in deciding how those assets were to be allocated. How were those extremely valuable commodities to be equitably distributed? Thus was born the high-stakes process that caught the attention of organized crime groups. And therein lay the rub. What resulted was chaos, violence, and wholesale theft. In some cases that theft took place with the acquiescence of Russia's new leaders.

Among Russia's new leaders were those who had voluntarily partnered with powerful criminal elements. Yet others were forced into those partnerships through threats and violence. In short, throughout the 1990s, Russia was the scene of an economic and political free-for-all that benefitted some beyond anyone's imagination and led to the ruin of others. And it didn't take long for the consequences of that chaos to land on the doorsteps of FBI offices across the US. In San Francisco two specific examples of how the collapse of the Soviet Union directly impacted the work of the FBI are laid out as follows:

Golden ADA: Among the former Soviet Union's treasured natural resources were precious metals and gems, including massive stores of rough, uncut diamonds that had been mined in the Soviet Union and were owned by the state. Under the new Russian Federation, the individual ultimately responsible for the handling and sale of these prized government assets was the director of the Russian Federation's Committee for Precious Metals and Gems (the "Committee"), who was appointed to that position with the blessings of Russia's newly minted president, Boris Yeltsin. So what happened to those extremely valuable assets? How did their value ultimately benefit the new citizens of Russia? (Spoiler alert: they didn't.)

In the early 1990s, the Committee established Golden ADA, a diamond-processing facility in San Francisco where tens of millions of dollars in rough diamonds were to be cut, polished, and sold, with the proceeds transferred back to the Russian government. But Golden ADA's Soviet-born owners caught the FBI's attention when they began spending lavishly on Bay Area luxury homes, yachts, cars, high-end properties, and a Gulfstream jet. As it turned out, Golden ADA had a rather unorthodox business strategy: take possession of the government-owned rough diamonds from Moscow, cut and polish the diamonds in San Francisco, sell them on the open market, and pocket the proceeds. Evidence suggests that Golden ADA owners then kicked back huge sums to the director of the Committee in Moscow and his associates. Did they have to worry about accountability or being arrested in Moscow? That was up to Russian law-enforcement authorities, whose leaders answered to the same person ultimately responsible for appointing the Committee's director in the first place: President Boris Yeltsin. And in classic style, one can safely assume that everyone in on the scheme got their share of the pie. In the end, following a joint investigation between the FBI and trusted investigators from the Russian Ministry of Internal Affairs (MVD), some of the highest-ranking Russian officials involved with Golden ADA were charged, convicted, and sentenced to prison in Russia, only to be pardoned soon after.[9] As for the San Francisco-based Golden ADA founders, one was convicted in a US court on IRS tax fraud charges. The principal subject fled to Greece, where he was arrested and later extradited to Russia.

Prime Minister Pavel Lazarenko: Pavel Lazarenko was prime minister of Ukraine (a former Soviet Republic) from 1996 to 1999. While in office, he remotely purchased a multimillion-dollar estate near San Francisco, once the home of comedian Eddie Murphy. But Lazarenko's first trip to see his new home did not go as planned: he was arrested the moment he set foot on US soil—the direct result of an intensive joint US-Ukrainian investigation led by a relentless young agent on my squad. That agent was assisted by FBI legal attachés and foreign law enforcement agencies throughout Europe and the Caribbean—most notably, the legal attaché in Kyiv, who, having no independent investigative authority in Ukraine, coordinated with Ukrainian authorities to provide US-based authorities with evidence of violations of US law.[10] During Lazarenko's trial US prosecutors were able to prove that Lazarenko used US and other financial institutions to launder millions of dollars in assets stolen from the government of Ukraine. And although Lazarenko, while prime minister, was devious enough to conceal his theft through complex international financial maneuvers, one of his big mistakes was the high-profile purchase of his California home. In the end, Lazarenko, a flight risk who was denied bail, spent months awaiting trial in a federal jail near San Francisco. Following his conviction on US charges of conspiracy and money laundering, Lazarenko spent years in California's Terminal Island Federal Prison, a far cry from the lavish California lifestyle he once envisioned.[11]

As these cases suggest, the FBI's approach to organized crime stretches well beyond the stereotypes with which we are all familiar: crimes associated with gambling, drugs, loan-sharking, labor racketeering, prostitution, and extortion. In fact, the FBI's perspective on organized crime is much broader and includes far-reaching enterprises that can stretch across continents. But regardless of geography, these criminal enterprises, supported by threats and violence, cannot operate without corrupt government officials and businessmen. As for corrupt businessmen, Russian criminal organizations were extorting Russian businesses on an epic scale, violently taking over newly created banks and businesses to launder the proceeds of their crimes—crimes that were fueled, in part, by the theft of the former Soviet Union's once state-owned assets. And the chaos and complicity within the administration of President Boris Yeltsin, the first democratically elected leader in Russian history and the new face of the Russian Bear, was making this all possible.

In the spring of 1998, I was offered a forty-five-day temporary duty assignment as assistant legal attaché (ALAT) Moscow, based in the US Embassy. I jumped on the offer with both feet. What better way to learn about the criminal organizations that had been our focus for the past three years? What better place to experience the "bear" up close and personal and, in the process, stretch the FBI's ability to connect with critical members of the Bay Area's Russian-speaking community? And what better time to watch history unfold—less than seven years after the collapse of the Soviet Union!

As in all legat assignments, I would join in coordinating with host-country law enforcement on overlapping, transnational criminal and terrorism investigations—cross-border partnerships that are essential to the FBI's mission given that, outside United States territory, FBI agents have no on-the-ground investigative authority, no powers of arrest, and no authority to carry firearms. In lieu of these powers, the FBI relies on mutually beneficial relationships with its host-country counterparts in foreign countries to obtain needed information in support of US-based investigations. My principal partners for this assignment would be criminal investigators from the Ministry of Internal Affairs (MVD), a Russian law enforcement agency with no built-in counterintelligence responsibilities and that is theoretically separate and apart from the former KGB.

As I prepared for my departure to Moscow, I had a sense of the transformation Russia was undergoing and how those changes fit into Russia's growing reputation as the Wild East. Among the most visible changes I expected to see was the rise of privileged, powerful, ultrawealthy oligarchs who relied on political connections and/or violence to keep their pockets full. I heard stories of New Russians who were flaunting their prosperity, buying up as much as they could, spending lavishly to announce their new wealth—a phenomenon encapsulated in a story about one New Russian who was overheard bragging to another about the cost of his new Rolex. His friend's boastful response? "That's nothing. I bought the same watch for *twice* the price!"[12] I expected to see evidence of this wealth in the new banks that were being built to protect and manage the huge sums of cash that flowed from both privatization and the proceeds of organized crime. And I heard stories of violent car bombings and assassinations, many directed at Russia's new bankers and journalists, who were among organized crime's prime targets. I also heard nightmarish accounts of the city's collapsing infrastructure—the result of government bureaucracies' inability to keep up with years of Soviet decay. Among the most gruesome consequences were sinkholes on sidewalks that literally swallowed unsuspecting pedestrians as they casually walked down the street, boiling them alive in the steam that ran through Moscow's underground hot-water-heating system.[13] And I was aware that the military, too, was faltering, as Soviet army paraphernalia was being sold by the carload at outdoor markets. But despite all that I had learned before my departure, I remained woefully unprepared for what I was about to experience.

After a childhood with Russia on my mind, which was punctuated by nuclear attack drills at school, civil defense films shown to us as cub scouts on the destructive power of "the bomb," and the Cuban Missile Crisis, followed by an adult preoccupation marked by détente, the fall of the Berlin Wall, the collapse of the Soviet Union, and the plausible absurdity of Dr. Strangelove, I was finally preparing to land at Moscow's Sherametyevo airport. As my headphones blasted Rachmaninov's Piano Concerto No. 3 in D Minor, I got my first glimpse of the dense forests around Moscow. It was surreal, to say the least.

One never gets a second chance to make a first impression, and neither does a city. As I traveled from the airport to my hotel, my first impression of Moscow was stark: the surroundings were dreary gray, just as they'd appeared in the black-and-white newsreel footage of Moscow my generation grew up with. And although dotted with modern structures, the landscape was blanketed with clusters of dingy gray, featureless, cookie-cutter high-rise apartment buildings that Soviet leader Leonid Brezhnev built in the 1970s—monuments to the Soviet communist ideal that no citizen (except for members of the Communist Party) should have any more than their neighbor, especially anything that resembled Western decadence. In the days to come, I would see more evidence of Moscow's decay: aged, poorly dressed babushkas (grandmothers) selling fresh-cut lilacs and cigarettes outside the entrances to Moscow's elegant metro system; they did so to survive the loss of buying power that sprang from the hyperinflation that was steadily wiping out their promised pensions. There were packs of feral dogs ("metro dogs") that roamed the streets and metro entrances by night and slept in packs by day. And there were the women who swept the sidewalks with homemade brooms made of bundled tree branches, not to mention the incapacitated veterans of the war in Afghanistan on makeshift crutches. All were symbols of communism's broken promise and the difficult transition to capitalism. But I would soon experience a series of far different, mind-blowing firsts that were all good.

My first venture out of my hotel was to a Western-style restaurant (Patio Pasta) on Tverskaya Street, one of the main arteries leading to Red Square. What were the first Russian words I uttered? "Pivo pozhaluista" (Beer please) to Igor the bartender—words that would later symbolize the challenge I would be giving my liver in the coming forty-five days. The next morning's agenda should not surprise any American who grew up during the Cold War: my first peek behind the curtain—a trip to Red Square.

It's hard to explain the emotions I felt with my first step onto Red Square. The word *surreal* hardly does the moment justice, and to be sure, I experienced an overwhelming sense of disbelief and irony. This was the setting I had seen so many times in old newsreels and documentaries, where imposing Soviet leaders clad in colorless shades of gray stood shoulder to shoulder on Lenin's mausoleum (pictured in figure 2.1), reviewing columns of soldiers, missiles and tanks, all of which had one mission: the annihilation of the Soviet Union's mortal enemy. (That would be us.) Here was Red Square, where every structure still screamed power, despite the fact that, in 1998, those screams sounded more like a distant echo. Here was St. Basil's Cathedral with its colorful onion domes—the symbol of the Russian Orthodox Church that was built by Ivan the Terrible to commemorate Russia's defeat of the Golden Horde invaders from the East. Adjacent to Red Square is the Kremlin, once the beating heart of Soviet authority. Central to Red Square is the mausoleum where, for decades, Russians have stood in line to view the now century-old body of Vladimir Ilyich Lenin, the hero of the Bolshevik Revolution who, in 1918, ordered the savage murder of the entire Russian royal family. Not far from Lenin is the Kremlin Wall Necropolis where

Figure 2.1. Lenin's Mausoleum, Red Square, 2005.
SOURCE: AUTHOR'S PERSONAL COLLECTION

Josef Stalin is buried, along with the nightmares of those he banished to forced labor camps (gulags) in Siberia and barren no-man's-lands in Central Asia. Not far from Stalin is the body of Felix Dzerzhinsky, "Iron Felix," the leader of what would one day become the KGB. Buried with Iron Felix are the horrors of those the KGB and its predecessor agencies brutally tortured and murdered at Lubyanka, the KGB's Moscow head-quarters. Looming above Red Square are the Kremlin Towers, topped by imposing red stars, symbols of the Soviet Union's military might. And looking up at all those haunting symbols of Soviet power from the cobblestone entrance to the square was a wide-eyed agent of the FBI—one of the KGB's historic US adversaries—who was in Moscow at the invitation of the Russian government. And hiding behind that FBI agent was the shadow of a scared kid, haunted by years of cowering under his desk during drills designed to simulate a Soviet nuclear attack. If only someone had told that child back in the 1950s and 1960s that someday, everything would be okay . . . at least for the moment!

My first trip on the magnificent Moscow Metro left another lasting impression, starting with the long (roughly three-minute) escalator rides that take passengers deep in and out of the metro's museum-like subway stations, each with a unique artistic theme and each a monument to Russian culture and communist ideology. Built deep underground to double as bomb shelters, metro stations service the clocklike trains that keep Moscow humming until they come to a full stop each night at 1:00 a.m. And since the long, slow-moving up and down escalators are adjacent to each other, they were the perfect place to people watch, which reliably included young Russian couples' carefree public displays of affection and the hollow, blank stares of their elders.

My next venture was the Kremlin Palace Theater, which was walking distance from Red Square, where a Sunday afternoon performance of *Swan Lake* was to take place. I was truly overcome by the majesty of the stage, the performers, and the music. It was nothing like I had ever experienced, despite my having attended many elegant performances at Chicago's world-class theaters. I was equally impressed by the young teenage boys and girls who were engrossed in the production—the same boys who later gathered in the bathroom for a smoke, leading me to conclude that, for young Russians, being cool and loving ballet were not mutually exclusive.

As I would soon learn, most Russians share a sense of pride in what they refer to as the Russian soul, a concept that, for me as an outsider, is akin to the mysteries of dark matter—intangible, elusive, and indefinable; vaguely discernible to me only through the creations of Russian artists. To my mind, I got my first glimpse into the heartwarming side of the Russian soul during the *Swan Lake* performance and, to a greater extent, at my next exploration.

The Moscow Conservatory, not far from Red Square, is where Sergei Rachmaninov and other world-famous composers and performers studied and where, upon its opening in 1866, Pyotr Tchaikovsky served as professor of theory and harmony. Since that time the Conservatory has been a platform for some of the world's most renowned musicians. And with walls adorned with images of history's greatest composers, it offers the audience a sense of intimacy, history, and connection to music's heroes, past and present. It was also the scene of my second attempt at speaking Russian: "Odin bilyet pozhaluista" (One ticket please).

Not surprisingly, the quality of the performance was world-class and elegantly represented one of the many cultural achievements of which Russians are so proud. How many times was I reminded of the preeminence of Russia's legendary artists: composers, musicians, dancers, painters, sculptors, poets, actors, and writers! What I experienced at the Conservatory fully embodied that claim as I watched a love affair unfold between the orchestra and its audience. This was a performance free from any barriers or a sense that the musicians were there to do a job, get paid, and go home. Instead, what I witnessed was a joyful audience-orchestra embrace, deeply affectionate and contagious, ending in passionate applause that was itself musical. It was also inspiring to watch small children emulate their musical heroes as they played imaginary keyboards on the railing in front of their seats. For me, this was a magical moment and an honor to be part of it.

These were just the first in a series of cultural thrills I would experience as the weeks went on, not the least of which were performances at venues such as the Bolshoi Theater. The elegance and beauty of the Bolshoi were overwhelming, and I later found myself attending productions I knew nothing about just to be in that grand setting. But the history of the Bolshoi stretched beyond its artistic notoriety into its significance as a symbol of Richard Nixon's 1972 breakthrough visit to Moscow; the trip that showcased his foreign policy genius and introduced my generation to the power of the word *détente*—an easing of tensions and an effort to bridge the huge gap in communications between the US and Soviet Union. And, to be sure, few experiences are more emblematic of the Russian soul than the performance of Tchaikovsky's *Swan Lake* that Nixon and the First Lady experienced during that visit.

But woven into the tortured tapestry, creativity, and artistic beauty that are synonymous with the enigmatic Russian soul are centuries of suffering; a painful history intertwined with the anguish of Ukrainians, Russian and Soviet Jews, Chechens, Kazakhs, Tatars, and many other Soviet ethnic and religious groups who, in some cases, agonized in far greater numbers than their Russian neighbors. Twentieth-century Soviet history is replete with heartbreaking tragedies, starting with the tens of thousands who were arrested, tortured, and murdered by leaders of the Bolshevik Revolution during the Red Terror of 1918; the millions of deaths from starvation following Stalin's program of agricultural "collectivization" in the 1930s; the hundreds of thousands who died under Stalin during the Great Purge of the 1930s; the twenty-seven million Soviets killed during World War II, including the millions of Russians who died from artillery fire and starvation during the Siege of Leningrad and the Battle of Stalingrad. Subsequent tragedies include the millions of Soviets who were exiled by Stalin to Siberia and Central Asia in the 1940s; the millions who perished during the famine of 1946–1947; and the many Soviet dissidents, such as novelist Aleksandr Solzhenitsyn, who were brutally tortured in Soviet gulags throughout much of Soviet history. Those ordeals were a continuation of a long line of historic nightmares, dating back to early Russian history with the thirteenth-century Mongol Golden Horde invasion, the Swedish invasion of Russia in 1708, Napoleon's failed nineteenth-century Russian conquest (the inspiration for Tchaikovsky's 1812 Overture), and the murder of thousands of Russian peasants at the hands of Tsar Nicholas II's palace guards in the early 1900s.

Soviet and Russian history are replete with tales of day-to-day, down-to-the-wire struggles for survival; some the product of brutal religious, ethnic, and political persecution, many at the hands of their own despotic leaders, but all accompanied by punishing cold and starvation. In the case of outside attacks, the effects of those onslaughts are baked into the Russian psyche, leaving many with a raw sense of vulnerability that is reflected in a preoccupation with walls: around the Kremlin, through the heart of Berlin, or written on faces in a crowd. That vulnerability is at times susceptible to being turned on its head, transformed into a close cousin of paranoia and stirred into punishing aggression by Russia's masters of fear and manipulation—autocrats who are happy to fulfill a devil's bargain in which Russians' personal freedoms and connection to the outside world are cashed in for a sense of stability and security, leaving them at the mercy of those brutal despots. The end result is a self-fulfilling prophecy in which a shared identity as victims leaves many Russians feeling isolated, threatened, and primed to lash out at apparitions dressed in enemy uniforms whose imaginary sights are set on the Kremlin.

The shared suffering associated with these tragedies, the struggle to agree on what it means to be "Russian" in a vast territory that has been buffeted for centuries between East and West, and the search for answers in their peasant roots and Orthodox heritage are among the inspirations for Russian poets, composers, painters, writers, and film directors as they seek color, comfort, and a way of making sense of this often-tumultuous world. In the movie *Moscow on the Hudson*, starring Robin Williams as a Soviet defector to the US, Williams's jazz-musician character offers insight into that world as he explains to a newfound American friend how he loves his misery—a contradiction in terms that, on its face, seems illogical. But loving one's misery may stem from the collective pride and defiance that springs from a society's ability to withstand and overcome some of the worst fates that have ever been thrown at one group of people, a sense of pride that is built into Russians' shared identity passed from generation to generation through household names such as Pushkin, Tolstoy, and Shostakovich.

"Step left, step right, get shot" (Шаг влево, шаг вправо, расстрел) is an expression that, for me, opened another window into Soviet thinking. Taught to me by a Russian colleague in San Francisco, the phrase may stem from accounts of life in Soviet gulags, where prisoners were brutally tortured whether or not they confessed to imaginary crimes. The phrase hints at feelings of helplessness, hopelessness, and resignation to one's fate that were ingrained in many former Soviet citizens. One guiding principle behind the expression is conformity, a mindset that the state instilled in Soviet citizens at an early age. This was a world in which people had limited power to shape their everyday lives, where a "one size fits all" lifestyle offered few choices, whether having to do with housing, education, careers, travel, or personal indulgences. It was a world in which falling out of lockstep, deviating from a predetermined path, and/or reaching outside of the box often flew in the face of communist teachings and, in some cases, crossed a line into Western decadence.[14] What was the end result? There was no need to worry about making choices; there weren't many. And when faced with a fork in the road, Soviet citizens found neither option was good. Left with a diminished capacity to make choices and control their future, they were often led to believe in the Russian proverb "There's no escape from fate" (От судьбы не уйти).

For some, that fate offered a painful lifetime path. One such person was a wheelchair-bound teenager who caught my attention as she shopped for souvenirs at the Kremlin Palace Theater gift shop. As the young woman quietly admired items in the display case, a saleswoman harshly and loudly scolded her in front of everyone. It was ugly, and in no way could I see anything that prompted the outburst. What a contrast to the beauty of the *Swan Lake* performance I had just experienced! I later learned some painful realities about being born disabled in the Soviet Union, where new mothers were given a stark choice: turn their newborns over to the state, to be hidden away and "cared for" in orphanages, or care for disabled children on their own with little support. Step left, step right, get shot.

CHAPTER 3

A Mile in Another Man's Shoes

LIKE EVERY PROFESSION, SOCIAL WORK IS DEFINED BY A SET OF CORE
values and demanding ethical standards that are incapsulated in rules
governing its members. One such principle is the recognition of the
importance of human relationships, not the least of which is the relationship between the social worker and his or her client(s). As I learned,
starting in my early days as a graduate student in social work, an important element of that principle is the practitioner's ability to listen and to
see the world through the eyes of the other.

In the years preceding my FBI career, seeing the world from the
point of view of the other meant seeing life through the eyes of patients
confined to a hospital psychiatric ward, teenagers subject to dysfunctional
families and gangs, and later, adult criminal defendants placed on a form
of probation by judges from the Cook County courts. In many cases,
learning to appreciate the perspective of my clients was a serious challenge for a young man who had grown up in the blue-collar, lily-white
suburbs and later found himself knocking on doors, alone (and petrified),
in Chicago's poorest and most downtrodden neighborhoods and housing
projects. In the words of a coworker, son of a Mississippi sharecropper
and lifelong friend who grew up in those neighborhoods, I was a "fly in
buttermilk," the only white face for blocks in any direction. As such, I
was forced to address some ugly personal prejudices and to appreciate
life from the perspective of people who lived in a completely different
world than mine. And as a young graduate student interning as a social
worker in a suburban police department, my values were again impacted

by people who saw the world far differently than I. This time it would be police officers whom I grew to respect, whose worldview reflected the pain and frustration of repeatedly dealing with innocent victims of senseless crimes.

Changes in my thinking came to a head during my last years as a caseworker for the criminal courts, where my peers included fellow social workers, young psychologists, and a handful of former Catholic priests. Our job was to supervise adult criminal offenders and, through counseling and other support services, help them break the cycle of recidivism. Changes in my outlook stemmed in part from the criminal background checks we conducted on each client prior to our initial meeting. All too often, those old-style, computerized arrest records unfolded like paper accordions, stretching the length of the long hallway outside our office doors—a ritual that could be exhausting and disheartening. After years of that scenario, I found the emotional fatigue had run its course, leading me to search for a new career. But despite my frustrations with social work, the ability to put myself in the place of the other was a skill that later helped me open my eyes to a new and fascinating Russian world.

Lest I give the impression that my Moscow life was centered on concerts, the ballet, and sightseeing, I should say that workdays were long and challenging. I was learning the basic drill: how to convey US-based FBI requests to the Russians and how to direct investigative requests of the Russians to FBI field offices. As part of my duties, I interacted on a regular basis with a broad range of Russian officials: police investigators, judges, and prosecutors—a group that I once would have casually dismissed as the other. These were the people whom we in the free world once collectively referred to as "Commies," a demeaning epithet designed to dehumanize our adversary, much like people throughout history have branded their enemies with an array of racist, ethnic, political, and religious slurs. Doing so is an age-old survival tool that has been used by adversaries to weaponize hatred for the other and insulate themselves from collective guilt should they witness or cause the suffering of a group they consider evil, morally inferior, or less than human. And so I began to appreciate the price we pay for dismissing an entire group of people with a derogatory slur. For me, the bottom line was this: of all the experiences that came with my Moscow assignment, rehumanizing the other, which included seeing the world through the eyes of my Russian colleagues, was the most meaningful and, in truth, the most personally fulfilling.

In some ways, my Russian counterparts and I were cut from the same cloth. We all grew up in fear of nuclear war, carnage, and destruction as we practiced so-called survival drills under our desks or in school hallways, our heads buried between our legs under the ludicrous presumption that doing so would protect us from a nuclear inferno. Like my family, my Russian counterparts were sure to have had supplies of food stashed away to help them survive the aftermath of a nuclear attack. (Right!) And we all knew our path to the nearest form of shelter, however pitifully inadequate. For all of us, these were feel-good measures that afforded us little benefit beyond the illusion of safety. And with those drills as our backdrop, each side experienced the Cuban Missile Crisis from a different vantage point. In our case, we faced a theoretical doomsday scenario stemming from Soviet nuclear warheads secreted ninety miles from our border. For the more senior of my new Russian colleagues and all their surviving parents, their nightmares had a far different point of reference: Hitler's invasion and the deadly assaults that mobilized the entire Soviet population—men, women, and children—ending in wholesale destruction, unspeakable atrocities, and the death of tens of millions of friends, family, and fellow citizens in their backyards.

Despite the collapse of the Soviet Union, my Russian counterparts maintained pride in their heritage, culture, and historic achievements. Their national self-image included the firm conviction that the Soviet Union was uniquely responsible for Germany's defeat in the Great Patriotic War (World War II) and their belief in the historic prowess of Russian Olympic athletes. Their "firsts" in space were another source of pride: the first satellite to orbit the earth (Sputnik) and the first man in space (Yuri Gagarin). But in vivid contrast to their proud past, life in the (1990s) present was a disaster, defined by a devastating financial crisis, political chaos, and widespread violence—all catastrophic blows to their national pride. And along with their Cold War defeat came the loss of their cherished superpower status, the biggest blow of all to their pride and place on the world stage.

In retrospect, I consider myself fortunate that my initial introduction to my Russian colleagues took place at a time (1998) when an open window had temporarily replaced a door slammed shut. What I experienced in that moment was a peek into the Russian soul and, for the blink of an eye, a feeling of optimism on both sides. During that fleeting moment, those of us representing the FBI and our Russian partners could let our hair down and even become friends (not that we would say that out loud) and yet remain faithful to our respective countries. Though I am sure that feeling is now in a deep coma, that was a time to let the air out of a lifetime of fear of the other. But before *fully* exhaling, I took one last shot at purging my Cold War demons.

"If the shoe doesn't fit . . . " Novodevichy Cemetery is one of Moscow's most sacred places, where many Russian and Soviet cultural heroes—political leaders, leading scientists, military heroes, writers, poets, and film stars—are buried. There lie so many icons of Russian history, each with a unique and beautiful monument to honor the reverence and memory of those historic figures. It is located on the grounds of Novodevichy Convent, where Russian tsars were known to banish their ex-wives (and relatives) as they went in search of their future ex-wife. But for me, as an American who grew up in the heat of the Cold War, the monument that evoked the most haunting memories sat atop the grave of Nikita Khrushchev—the former leader of the Soviet Union who, on October 12, 1960, famously scared the s—t out of me and everyone I knew by (allegedly) banging his shoe on his desk at the United Nations, an event that would forever remain linked to his threat in 1956 to bury capitalism and, by extension, the United States. Of all the well-known Cold War images, that portrayal of Khrushchev at the United Nations, whether fact or fiction, was, for me, the most disturbing.

Operation Shoe was what we called it. In theory, it might also be described as an act of adolescent acting out or as irresponsible, unprofessional, utterly undiplomatic, and definitely dangerous. In today's annoying psychobabble, we might call it closure. But at its core, the simple act of holding a shoe above Khrushchev's grave was my middle finger to years of childhood fears and payback for that day in October 1960, when wielding a shoe had the power to terrify an entire generation of kids just like me.

Nearly four decades after Khrushchev's threat to bury the capitalist West, the thaw in tensions that followed the collapse of the Soviet Union paved the way for the 1994 agreement between the US and Russian governments to open a permanent FBI office on Russian territory. The opening of the legat office in Moscow can largely be attributed to a push by former FBI director Louis Freeh, a visionary who clearly saw the value in formalizing cooperation between the FBI and Russian law enforcement. With this development, investigators from each side had a platform where they could meet face-to-face and exchange investigative requests, enhancing their ability to collaborate on overlapping criminal and terrorism investigations. But despite this developing win-win partnership, one had to bear in mind that Russian law enforcement's less visible counterpart, the KGB, had not simply faded away.

When I arrived in Moscow in 1998, the legat office was in a maze of US Embassy structures then under construction. Years earlier, construction of a new multistory embassy building had begun, using Soviet laborers. But in 1998, the US was in the process of tearing down the top floors of that same building and replacing them with a new, secure structure, complete with all the bells and whistles. Of course, the new embassy building was being built not only as a base for routine, unclassified functions but also to house classified information and equipment. It was also a base for analysis of intelligence information. So why was it necessary to tear down and rebuild? Because under the KGB's guidance, Soviet "laborers" had built the original structure with a few bells and whistles of their own—dozens of listening devices embedded in the walls that were discovered by the State Department in 1985.[1] As a result, US engineers rebuilt the top floors of the embassy using cleared American construction workers and materials shipped to Moscow under armed guard. The new structure was eventually completed in 2000.[2]

Having worked organized crime for many years, I came to appreciate the investigative power of electric surveillance. I also understood the value of informants who were willing to betray criminal organizations to which they had once been loyal. To put things in perspective, my time in

Moscow was four years after the arrest of CIA officer Aldrich Ames, a double agent who was convicted of clandestinely working for the KGB and was allegedly responsible for the death of numerous Soviet defectors working for the CIA.[3] Several years earlier, the FBI had uncovered another spy in the midst of the US intelligence community—a Los Angeles-based FBI agent who was charged with espionage after an adulterous affair with a woman later determined to be a Soviet agent. And upon my arrival in Moscow, I learned the story behind a member of the US Marine Security Guard—an elite group of US Marines posted to US embassies throughout the world whose mission includes protection of embassy personnel and guarding access to classified documents and equipment. That Marine Corps sergeant had been posted to Moscow in the 1980s when, like the Los Angeles-based FBI agent, he, too, provided classified information to a young Russian lover who was later exposed as a KGB officer, leading to his conviction on espionage charges in 1987. Given that recent history, I understood that the Federal Security Service (FSB)—the principal organization that arose from the ashes of the KGB's dissolution in 1991—was still out there, in search of blood in the water.

CHAPTER 4

When Truth Is a Menace

"[THERE IS] ONE IRON RULE: LOGIC IS AN ENEMY AND TRUTH IS A MEN-ace" is a line from a *Twilight Zone* episode ("The Obsolete Man") that touches on the fallacies those of us from both East and West grew up with during the Cold War. The story is centered on a futuristic, dystopian society where books are a threat, and a librarian whose services are no longer needed is condemned to death. In that world, "truth" is defined by the state, and the truths found in books, especially those that challenge state propaganda, are a menace.

As children growing up in the 1950s and 1960s, we were fed a distorted image of the Soviet Union that was, in part, a product of Western propaganda. In that version of truth, all Soviets were warmongers, single-minded in their lust to spread their toxic communist beliefs at any cost. Theirs was a frigid, empty, black-and-white world, where no one smiled, and no one had anything to smile about. They were atheists who were devoid of a human spirit and a moral compass and who, lacking spiritual guidance, followed their despotic leaders like sheep. And in that bleak and barren world, there was no hope and no future. In that version of truth, Westerners were righteous and morally superior and owned the future, while the Evil Empire was condemned to remain locked in the past and fail.

Soviet citizens were also victims of their own Cold War propaganda, wholly convinced of the superiority of communism and the abject failures of Western capitalism, leading them to believe that nowhere in the world was life better than in the Soviet Union. Were their beliefs based on logic and truth? In fact, Soviet citizens were getting a highly distorted picture both of themselves and the other—a product of the Communist Party's restrictions on exposure to foreigners and foreign travel, book bans, and internal control of the media and artistic expression, allowing only a positive portrayal of Soviet life and a lopsided focus on America's struggles with racism, poverty, and ghettos.

One telltale story, told to me by a veteran CIA intelligence officer, focused on a Russian official's first trip to the US around the time of the dissolution of the Soviet Union. Like his countrymen, that individual was familiar with the struggles common to everyday Soviet life, and yet he believed that a failing US system was worse. Thus was born a debate between two natural adversaries, both of whom believed in the superiority of their respective socioeconomic and political systems. To settle the debate, the Russian official requested a tour of typical American neighborhoods, including a trip to a local supermarket, where he was confident he would find the same empty shelves and long lines that he was used to at home. We know the outcome: the store was well stocked with a wide variety of food and other necessities, minus the endless lines, grim faces, and lack of choices to which he was accustomed. Claiming that the store to which he had been taken was a setup, the Russian official continued to challenge the CIA officer. What was his response? "OK, we'll drive around, wherever you say, and visit any grocery store you choose." And for a second time, the Russian official came face-to-face with the Soviet-fed fiction he had always swallowed. His deflated response? "They lied!" His utter sense of betrayal and disillusionment with communist leaders was exposed and would one day become fertile ground for the US intelligence community's recruitment of well-placed sources within powerful Russian institutions.

But Russians were not the only ones forced to confront preconceived notions about the "other." My assumption that all Russian men were soulless, warmongering alcoholics who were married to uneducated, semitoothless women, banished to a life of hard labor in factories and collective farms faced its own reckoning in 1998.[1] What I experienced flew squarely in the face of the unflattering, Western-serving stereotypes I grew up with. My new Russian colleagues were engaging, warm, and welcoming, rich with humor, lovers of poetry, and insightful observers of human nature. They offered their hand in friendship, seeming to thoroughly enjoy sharing stories and anecdotes about Russian culture and learning about the real United States. The women I met were poised, self-assured, and well educated, and they could discuss English- language literature far more fluently than I. My first walks down Moscow's main thoroughfares were a revelation of another sort: women dressed fashionably and elegantly—no jeans, no sweatshirts, no sneakers. Eye contact was easy, and smiles were plentiful. It was what my partner and I rather irreverently referred to as the "all day, everyday parade of swans." And what remained of those childhood stereotypes evaporated the first time I watched a soulful young Russian woman gracefully cover her head as she lit a candle and said a prayer in a Russian Orthodox church in the southwestern city of Taganrog.

In contrast to its soulful beauty, there was a disquieting flip side to Moscow, which was best captured in the Russian expression "Everyone has their own cockroaches" (У каждого свои тараканы). This alternate universe was a shadowy world inhabited by well-dressed, black-clad thugs, who came out at night and lurked around any venue that smelled like money: casinos, nightclubs, upscale hotels, and restaurants. In the late 1990s, their trademark vehicle was the luxury Mercedes jeep—seemingly built to intimidate, usually black, and with an air of power and superiority. Those vehicles cautiously cruised streets known for car bombings, violence among rival criminal gangs, and attacks on wealthy businessmen. As they did so, they traveled alongside the broken down, rusted-out Soviet Ladas, Zhigulis, and Moskvitches that few Russians could afford and that those who could had waited years to buy. It was all about power, and the streets were a testament to the fact that, in Moscow, there was no middle ground; one either had it or they didn't. It was also common to see high-end vehicles equipped with blue emergency lights. Like the Mercedes jeeps, those vehicles had an air of privilege and superiority as drivers used the flashing lights to barrel their way through Moscow's choking traffic and, at the same time, implicitly warn traffic police, other drivers, and pedestrians that the occupants had powerful connections.

For newcomers to Moscow, sidewalks presented their own perils. Soon after my arrival in Moscow, I was alerted to situations that may appear innocent, especially to Western visitors, but may in fact be fraught with danger. So imagine you are an American tourist strolling down the streets of central Moscow, awed by your novel surroundings. In front of you, you have observed a pedestrian who casually reached into his or her pocket and unknowingly dropped a wad of cash. What would you do? You basically have three options: (a) you ignore what you just saw and keep walking; (b) you pick up the money and discreetly place it in your pocket; or (c) you reach down, pick up the money, and politely hand it to the person who dropped it. My guess? Many Americans would choose a version of option *c*. But if your answer was anything but *a*, you just stepped into a classic Russian mousetrap. What you didn't see was the man with a badge (real or otherwise) who approaches you after being alerted by the "victim" who dropped the money. The victim has accused you of being a pickpocket (a common problem in Moscow). Remember! Unless you ignored what you saw, you are likely said to have some link to the "victim's" money. Of course, you were just trying to do the right thing, but no matter how much you protest, the situation gets further and further out of hand. Ultimately, you are placed under arrest by the man with the badge, who has offered you the chance to pay your fine on the spot. So you'd have to ask yourself, How much would I, the American novice, be willing to pay to stay out of a Russian jail?

In those days Moscow was also home to roving gangs of Nazi skin-heads—street gangs composed of racist thugs who preyed on minorities, especially Blacks and migrant workers from Central Asia and Chechnya. Skinheads were a very threatening group, who brazenly advertised their antisocial culture in the form of public rallies. In May 1998, soon after my arrival in Moscow, four skinheads severely beat a Marine attached to the US Marine Security Guard, a Black man, as he and a female companion were shopping at an outdoor market.[2] Skinheads also preyed on homosexuals, who got little sympathy in a country where some steadfastly have denied their existence in Russia, and where those who acknowledged homosexuality's existence generally held their lifestyle in contempt.

Among Western expats there was a popular English-language newspaper known as the *Exile*, where one could read truly dark stories about Moscow's underbelly. Articles tended to focus on a side of Moscow one would never find in tourist travel guides or the English-language *Moscow Times*. Instead, the *Exile* articles centered on scenarios not typically found in the West, with a uniquely Russian undertone. Among the features were critical reviews of popular venues—upscale nightclubs and bars—some of which had well-earned reputations for over-the-top debauchery. Based on the visual four-star reviews to which we are accustomed in the US, the *Exile* had a unique rating system to predict the likelihood of expats getting beat up or sexually satisfied (or both) at specific venues. In lieu of stars, the *Exile* used drawings of thugs (crew cuts and intimidating faces); the number of thugs (from one to four) depicted the likelihood of exiting an establishment with lumps on one's head. The likelihood of an evening ending in sexual intercourse was represented by stick figures in sexually explicit poses. In either category, four "stars" represented a near-sure bet. As the comedian Yakov Smirnoff used to say, "What a country!"[3]

Despite the stories and for reasons I still can't explain, I did not feel threatened on Moscow streets, nor did I have any real concerns about taking the metro late into the night. Was I bulletproof? Certainly not. Maybe it was because the streets were generally crowded late into the evening. Or maybe I just had a false sense of security in the belief that my hosts might be quietly tracking me. Having said that, I found that the most dangerous thing one could do in Moscow was cross the street, as one was required to navigate streets filled with aggressive drivers who had little or no regard for pedestrian safety. In some cases one could avoid that challenge by crossing the street using *perekhods* (underground pedestrian tunnels), where one was often entertained by extremely talented musicians. But in other locations, one was stuck trying to dodge privileged drivers who clearly had no respect for pedestrians. My theory was that, for Muscovites, owning a car symbolized superior social status, which afforded drivers the right to expect everyone to get out of their way. It was not pretty and was emblematic of a general disregard for personal safety that permeated day-to-day life in Moscow.

For some, Moscow sidewalks presented hazards of a different sort: small kiosks where a variety of items were sold, including alcohol. In those days it was not uncommon to see people casually strolling along the streets with bottles of Baltika beer or cans labeled "Vodka" as they made their way to the nearest McDonald's, the Conservatory, or Pushkin Square. Clearly, there was no taboo against drinking in public. As for me, I came to Moscow no stranger to alcohol, known on occasion to indulge in a "work hard, play hard" philosophy. But my past experience did not fully prepare me for just how far down the rabbit hole I was capable of going. And yes, I had good trainers!

Life in legat land is largely built on developing trusting relationships with host country counterparts. Among the first steps in that process is creating an atmosphere in which both sides get to know and grow comfortable with their new professional partners. Obviously, the better each side knows and trusts the other, the more likely it is that each will be able to secure needed help and thus get the job done. Each side's ability and willingness to provide the other with reliable investigative responses in a timely fashion is the most essential aspect of cementing that bond. But with the Russians, an unavoidable part of that process often included conferences that were followed by social gatherings centered on rituals built on the consumption of vodka.

I was introduced to those rituals in 1998, not long after my arrival in Moscow, when I flew to Rostov-on-Don, a city in the southwest of Russia, near Ukraine and the politically turbulent Northern Caucasus. This was a business trip sponsored by the American Bar Association's Central European and Eurasian Law Initiative (ABA-CEELI) that included presentations at the regional Ministry of Internal Affairs (MVD) Academy. Our small American delegation included a US district court judge, two prosecutors, and me. Our mission was to expose Russian judges, prosecutors, and law enforcement officials to the US judicial system and, in so doing, serve as a model for future Russian judicial reforms. The principal audience for this trip was a group of MVD recruits, among whom was a large contingent of young women dressed in their newly issued MVD short skirts and military-style hats. The day's presentations included discussions about how federal judges, prosecutors, and FBI agents interact and a presentation on the Racketeer Influenced Corrupt Organization (RICO) statute, US law enforcement's principal tool in fighting organized crime. For their part, the Russian presentations went into excruciating detail about a notorious serial killer from the region who brutally murdered several young women, evoking painful winces from the young recruits as the Russian presenter seemingly took delight in vividly describing the gruesome atrocities committed by this deranged man. But the daytime events were just a prelude to all that the MVD would teach us by evening. And as I would soon realize, there was a lot to learn.

Drinking with Russians in official settings was not characterized by a group of people casually sharing cocktails, belting down bottles of beer, or gently sipping fine wine over clever conversation. Rather, it centered on a series of back-and-forth, somewhat ritualized toasts that were punctuated with sips and, in some cases, full shots of vodka. In this ritual the group, usually standing, always drank "to" something and only when taking part in a toast. And you, dear readers, would be amazed how many things there were to toast to! The ritual was always initiated by the most senior Russian host, who opened the proceedings with an introductory welcome. I would describe this as an ice-breaking hospitality toast, which usually included a little about the host's venue and some emphasis on building good relations. In answer to the opening toast, it was incumbent upon a ranking member of the guests' delegation to reciprocate, which usually included a warm "thank you" and some happy horses—t (diplomatic, flowery language) about how much he was looking forward to this new relationship.

From that point the rules were ambiguous. The next toasts could be to the shared mission, to a developing friendship, or some other ode to success. After the opening toasts, the host generally moved on to new topics, which were answered by rotating members of the guests' delegation. At that point the evening could go almost anywhere, but at some point, within this shared law enforcement community, there was a traditional tribute to fallen comrades. And that's when things got dicey.

There were cases in which all sipped from their *rumkas* (shot glasses), but there were instances in which, out of respect, all were expected to drink *do dna* (to the bottom of the glass). This was true when toasting fallen comrades and women or, later, when toasting anything the presenter wished to emphasize as particularly important.[4] But there was one special circumstance, an especially important toast to a beloved woman (or women in general), in which the toaster challenged everyone to drink not only *do dna* but from a rumka balanced on the back of his hand. If one was able to do so without spilling a drop (or dropping the glass on the floor), it was a sign of a true commitment to the sentiment behind the toast.

Once everyone was sufficiently lubricated, the anecdotes and jokes began to flow (especially from the Russian side), along with more vodka. Many of the anecdotes centered on clever, ironic, or hilarious observations about politics and human nature. On the Russian side, there were no cultural guardrails to which we, as Americans, are accustomed. Russian anecdotes would be laced with racist and/or sexist references, and it was always fascinating to watch the wheels spin and the steam come out of Americans' ears as they weaseled their way into (or out of) a politically correct response: should they insult the host by not laughing, point out that Americans frown on that type of humor, or offer up a deep belly laugh, followed by a self-conscious attempt at recovery for the benefit of their American peers and the dubious assertion that they simply laughed out of politeness?

One of my favorite anecdotes was told by a Russian official who ridiculed Mikhail Gorbachev's futile efforts to discourage Russians from drinking alcohol. In so doing, Gorbachev was said to have cited experiments conducted by the Soviet Union's most accomplished scientists. According to the story, Gorbachev's scientists were able to prove that worms dropped in water live much longer than worms dropped in vodka, thus demonstrating the detrimental effects of alcohol. As the official raised his glass, he concluded his toast: "Here's to killing our worms." And so the evening and the toasts went on and on . . . (You get the point.) And in case anyone is wondering, pretending to sip is a challenge. The Russians are well versed in that bit of subterfuge, and all Russian eyes eventually fall on the guests to see how well they are playing the game. See figure 4.1 for an example of a Soviet anti-alcohol poster.

Figure 4.1.Soviet-Era Anti-Alcohol Poster.

"Never bleed around sharks" was one of the first bits of wisdom I picked up as a young FBI agent, an admonition against displaying insult or injury when fellow agents sought out and chipped away at one's weaknesses or sensitive underbelly in front of other agents. This is (or was) a survival tool within FBI culture that served to toughen young agents, who were learning that showing vulnerability when confronting lawbreakers on the street or defense attorneys in court was the surest way to end up facedown (literally and/or figuratively). It was a test we all faced, a rite of passage that was expected of us by seasoned, hardened street agents that I also bore in mind when building relationships with my Russian colleagues. This is not to say that the Russians were confrontative. In fact, our hosts generally treated us very respectfully. But drinking was a way for them to test us as men. (In those days, Russian law enforcement culture tended to only consider men as acceptable partners.) And as you might imagine, drinking like a "man" can take one to dark places.

My next business trip was to Krasnoyarsk, a city in Russian Siberia, where, in May 1998, I was again a member of a small delegation representing the US judicial system. Like with the trip to Rostov, this conference was sponsored by ABA-CEELI (American Bar Association, Central European and Eurasian Law Initiative) and was again composed of a US district court judge, two prosecutors, and me. After a long day of presentations on both sides, it was time to relax and get acquainted with our Russian hosts.

We were greeted that evening by a delegation of Russian judges in a private setting with a long, elegant table generously dressed with traditional Russian delicacies (including caviar) and, of course, an empty rumka at each place setting. Also strategically placed around the table were bottles of vodka that were handled only by the uniformed female servers, who made sure we *never* had so much as a half-empty glass (or a glass filled with water). We were off to the races!

As the evening wore on (and on . . .), I could feel myself responding to my inner never-bleed-around-sharks self. I kept up, along with my Russian colleagues, until the wee hours of the morning. This was not pretty, but how was I to put a merciful end to this future headache and yet save face? I challenged our hosts to join me in an early morning run.

So ended the evening, but as promised, right at the appointed time, the fiddler was standing at the foot of my bed with his hand out, demanding that I keep my end of the bargain and pay for the previous night's dance. Also nearby was the mirror that, without mercy, reminded me of the damage I had done to myself only a few short hours before—a scenario that might well have been the inspiration for the Russian expression "Don't blame the mirror because you're ugly" (Не пеняй на зеркало, коли рожа крива). And the next thing I remember was my painful attempt to purge the demons as my prosecutor partner and I jogged along the Yenisei River early on a snowy Siberian morning, a wake-up call in the truest sense. And how did the rest of the day go you ask? Another morning of presentations was followed by another round of lunchtime toasts.

The next day, I had my first experience as an unexpected guest on Russian television, which, for an FBI agent, is akin to touching the third rail. Following a meeting with a group of Russian investigators, I was ambushed by a local television crew with microphone and camera in hand. This was an uncomfortable situation on several levels, not the least of which was the fact that I was wearing a Communist Party pin that one of my Russian colleagues had earlier placed on my lapel. (Once again, never bleed around sharks!) The interviewer immediately attempted to corner me on live television with respect to a high-profile, controversial governor's race that was then underway. It was time to tap dance! First I immediately and subtly removed my lapel pin, lest some American somewhere take me for a communist sympathizer. Then came my response: "Those of us in the United States are very excited about *all* the changes taking place in Russia." And that was from the heart.

It's a fair question to ask whether all those belly laughs, overstuffed stomachs, and anesthetized brain cells actually helped accomplish the goal of building and nurturing working relationships with the Russians. (Remember that?) When all was said and done, it's hard to say, and I'll never really know for sure. But one thing *is* for sure: at least I killed my worms!

CHAPTER 5

Without Hard Work, One Can't Even Get a Fish Out of a Pond

Без труда не вытащишь и рыбку из пруда

MERRIAM-WEBSTER DEFINES CLUSTERF—K AS "A COMPLEX AND UTTERLY disordered and mismanaged situation: a muddled mess." And I'm here to tell you, muddled messes were a regular occurrence in Moscow. Day-to-day life never unfolded without a wrinkle or two, with chaos and dysfunction, obstacles to overcome, a puzzle to solve, or a knot to untie—so much so that my partner and I began tallying each incident in a futile attempt to keep a running total. Why that was, I'm not sure, but however one defines that invisible glue that binds a society together, enabling it to get things done—that glue was in short supply. At its core, rather than a well-oiled machine, this was a system gummed up by strangling bureaucracies, crippling corruption, and an inherent resistance to coming together to solve a problem. And despite Russian culture's wonderous achievements, it was crystal clear to me that Russian society was not designed for efficiency, a realization that left my partner and I shaking our heads, struggling to understand how the Soviets were able to come together to put the first man in space or build a military supposedly capable of threatening the Western world. It just didn't add up.

As we lifted the veil on Russian inefficiency, it became clear that nothing in Moscow was going to be simple. At first just figuring out how to pay for anything was a challenge. It didn't take long for my partner and

I to figure out that we needed exact change at every venue: restaurants, museums, tours, and performances. For some reason, no cashier ever had change, and it was almost amusing to watch the smoke come out of peoples' ears when handed a large bill. There was panic. And in those days, the obvious solution in our world (credit cards) was not an option.

Locating basic necessities was another challenge, requiring advanced planning and getting the lay of the land. Finding public restrooms was a perfect example, and although nice hotels and restaurants were generally reliable, traveling outside of the center of Moscow was another story. During a weekend trip to a quaint region outside of Moscow known for its medieval wooden churches (Suzdal), I asked a passerby where I might find a public toilet. He pointed to the surrounding landscape. I got the message. Another memorable moment centered on a weekend trip to St. Petersburg via the overnight train from Moscow. That was a harsh lesson, as my partner and I found ourselves, along with a collection of empty beer bottles, locked into our toilet-free four-person sleeper cabin. As we later learned, locking the doors from the outside at midnight was the standard procedure that was put into place to discourage thieves known to roam the train at night. This was a clear dilemma with no dignified solution. And no matter where we went, once we found a restroom, finding toilet paper was another hurdle, even at such elegant venues as the Bolshoi Theater. As a result, I quickly developed the habit of carrying a pocketful of hotel toilet paper wherever I went. But for those Bolshoi attendees lacking such foresight (especially Western tourists), I often wondered how they dealt with an unanticipated case of "royal family revenge."

Shopping was also complicated. To purchase gifts of any significant value (perfume, soaps, jewelry), one first had to choose the item from a display case. If the customer decided to buy, the saleswoman handed him or her a slip of paper describing the item and its price. From there, the buyer had to take the slip of paper to a cashier, where he or she paid for the item (in exact change in cash). The cashier would then hand the buyer a receipt, which had to be taken back to the grim-faced saleswoman. Only then could the buyer take possession of the item. Cumbersome as it was, the system worked, assuming one did not have to deal with separate lines at each step.

Lines were always a frustration, especially when there were none. In place of orderly lines, there was often a crush of densely packed people slowly but impatiently pushing their way into whatever entrance, cashier, or workstation they were trying to reach. In some cases reaching that destination ahead of others depended on one's willingness to pay a gate-keeper a few rubles. The lack of orderly lines was especially problematic at airports, where, upon landing, swarms of people anxiously pushed their way toward passport control and elbowed their way to their baggage. And just when arriving passengers thought they were in the clear, they were forced to steer their way through a gauntlet of private taxi drivers, all screaming "Toksi!" in unison. For departing passengers, their painful preflight hurdles included navigating frustrated crowds waiting to enter the airport, crowds waiting to have their baggage searched, crowds at check-in counters, and crowds of passengers attempting to form lines as they waited to board their plane. And when I say *lines*, I am using the term loosely. Adding insult to injury were the clearly miserable airport personnel who had the thankless job of controlling the chaos.

Among those known to solicit bribes on the street were MVD and other uniformed officers, some whose authority I never understood. Uniformed officers, carefully watching what people were doing, were everywhere. Many had a less-than-gentle way of dealing with the public. One former legat told me of an incident in which, after crossing the street outside of a designated crosswalk, he was promptly confronted by an MVD officer and punched in the face. That was, of course, before he had the opportunity to inform the officer of his diplomatic status.

One example of a true muddled mess is a situation I witnessed more than once: traffic jams, especially those caused by malfunctioning stoplights at busy intersections. To me, those situations were a perfect metaphor for a broken Soviet system in which ordinary citizens were unwilling or unable to work together to solve a problem. What do we do in the US if we come to blinking red traffic lights, signaling that the lights are out? We treat it as a stop sign. As a rule, every driver takes his or her turn in an orderly fashion, allowing the first driver who arrives at the intersection to proceed. And what is there to do if two vehicles arrive at the intersection simultaneously? We know the rule: the driver on the right has the right of way. Simple? Yes. Efficient? Indeed! And does everyone get through the intersection without wailing and gnashing of teeth? Usually. But what if there *are* no conventions? Or worse, what if everyone ignores the rules and charges ahead with no regard for the other guy, with an "I gotta get mine before the other guy gets his" attitude? There's chaos! A situation in which no one goes anywhere—a Gordian knot that further tightens with each approaching vehicle.

It begins with the first vehicles in the intersection vying to proceed ahead of each other. As they tangle in the middle of the intersection, filling every square inch of available space, they quickly lose the ability to go in reverse as cars behind them fill in the gap. This is the beginning of a mob mentality, a "me first" approach to a problem. And as more cars approach this tangled mess, they, too, make sure they get as close as possible to the car in front of them just in case the next guy tries to beat them through the intersection. What comes then? It becomes a large and growing knot of fuming drivers. Ultimately, this knot can only be untangled by a brave soul who gets out of his car and coaxes drivers out of their spaghetti-bowl creation.

Despite its many muddled messes, I couldn't wait to get back to Moscow. Maybe it was the unique nature of the work the FBI was doing in this novel environment. It might have been my fascination with Moscow's daily absurdities. It certainly could have been Moscow's energy, excitement, and rich culture. Or it may simply have been my craving for adventure. But one thing was for certain: after forty-five days, despite all the challenges, I wanted to go back, even as my appreciation for the US had grown by leaps and bounds. But what would be my professional path to get there? All roads went through Almaty, Kazakhstan, along with my first Russian language lessons.

CHAPTER 6

One Door Closes, Another One Opens

IN 2003 I APPLIED FOR THE POSITION OF LEGAL ATTACHÉ, ALMATY, Kazakhstan, a one-agent office that covered all of Central Asia and entailed frequent road trips to the other four Central Asian republics: Uzbekistan, Tajikistan, Kyrgyzstan, and Turkmenistan. Why did I choose Kazakhstan? Because as a Russian-speaking former Soviet country, it was a logical step toward my ultimate goal—legal attaché, Moscow. If selected for the Kazakhstan assignment, I would be faced with two hurdles: a polygraph administered through FBI Headquarters (FBIHQ) and an interview with FBI director Robert Mueller. As it turned out, I was tentatively approved for the job.

Of the two new challenges, the most intimidating was the polygraph, and since agent applicants weren't routinely polygraphed until years after I was hired, this would be my first. At the time I was hired, written tests, followed by intensive background checks by experienced agents, were among the first steps in determining an applicant's suitability. Next came face-to-face interviews with a panel of seasoned agents, who relied on their interviewing skills to delve into applicants' personal history and qualifications. Without polygraphs and highly scripted interviews, my impression was that, in those days, the panel's professional judgment carried significant weight in hiring decisions, allowing some flexibility to support those they believed to be qualified. Those qualifications favored applicants with an established career, a healthy dose of real-world life experience, and the ability to work effectively as a member of a team.

In my nineteen years, I had never taken a polygraph, a process that is unnerving under the best of circumstances.

The polygrapher was very professional and carefully walked me through the questions he intended to ask. I assume he did so to give me sufficient time to think about my answers and to heighten my anxiety. What impressed me most about this experience? Knowing that a lack of candor was a one-way ticket out of the FBI, I made sure my answers were entirely truthful. Having passed, my next hurdle was an interview with Director Mueller, who insisted on personally interviewing all agents who might soon be in charge of offices representing FBI interests overseas.

My interview with Director Mueller was relatively comfortable, largely due to his familiarity with the work of San Francisco's Russian Organized Crime squad. Prior to his appointment as FBI director in 2001, Robert Mueller III had been the United States Attorney in charge of all federal prosecutions in Northern California. Since his office had been a short elevator ride from the FBI office, we'd crossed paths frequently, and I'd gotten to know him professionally through my participation in negotiations with defense attorneys, including attorneys representing Pavel Lazarenko. He was an impressive leader, one whose charisma, character, and reputation as a balls-to-the-wall prosecutor and decorated Marine preceded him into any room. As the US Attorney, he was known to us as Bob, a name we would never consider uttering once he was appointed FBI director. Given our shared San Francisco background, I was hopeful that he would be comfortable green-lighting my Kazakhstan assignment, which he did.

Prior to setting out on long-term overseas assignments, future legats are provided predeployment training at the FBI Academy in Quantico, Virginia, an intensive one-week orientation that covers administrative procedures, the FBI's role in a US Embassy, counterintelligence concerns, and survival training. Despite my prior experience in Moscow, there was still much to learn for a street agent who had never before overseen an overseas FBI office.

The first aspect of my training was a readout on the cultural, political, and intelligence challenges I would face in Central Asia. That included a briefing at CIA headquarters in Langley, Virginia, by analysts whose job it was to know everything there was to know about their country of assignment. This was my first glimpse into working with the CIA, and I was wholly impressed with their grasp of minute details and their professionalism. I was also given a short briefing on my future intelligence community colleagues with whom I would be working on overlapping issues. To say that I was excited to meet these individuals is an understatement, and although the FBI and CIA historically had some difficulties cooperating, I was determined not to let this happen. (It didn't.)

Included in the training was a segment on the dangers of honeytraps, a low-budget, time-tested technique that has led to defections of government officials from all over the world. In the case of US Embassy personnel, honeytraps typically have involved a setup by a host-country intelligence agency to blackmail Americans—particularly those with access to classified information and/or in a position to influence US policy. The ruse begins with the target's new, seemingly innocent acquaintance with an attractive woman (or man, depending on circumstances). The most vulnerable target is a married man who is pressured to reveal government secrets after sexual contact with a person he is later shocked to discover is working with or as a foreign agent (pictures included). As I learned, officers of Kazakhstan's powerful intelligence service—the Committee for National Security (KNB)—were experts in such techniques, having originally been trained as KGB officers during Soviet times. (This was true of all the senior former Soviet intelligence officers with whom I worked in the five Central Asian countries.)

Other aspects of our training included exercises designed to heighten awareness of our surroundings and improve our reactions to situations that could threaten our safety. If not for the deadly serious nature of this training, these exercises would have been great fun. Exercises designed to enhance our ability to detect physical surveillance included scenarios in which we drove randomly in both rural and congested areas, tasked with detecting teams of expert FBI personnel who were assigned to clandestinely follow us. These were the "pros from Dover," whose day job was to remain invisible while tracking suspected spies from hostile countries who were operating in the Washington, DC, area. The goal of these exercises was to enhance our ability to detect the type of surveillance we could expect from host-country intelligence services and/or would-be terrorists. The last course of the training was a wakeup call: defensive driving, which was premised on being attacked by terrorists in one's overseas vehicle. The training included crashing through barriers at high speed, driving from the passenger's seat in the event one's driver was killed, controlling spinouts created when another car intentionally crashes into ours, and evasive driving—making split-second lane changes at high speed. And so the realities of life in our new world were rapidly coming into focus.

After my training and just prior to my deployment, I was invited to a meeting between Director Mueller and one of Kazakhstan's most powerful officials, KNB chairman Nartai Dutbayev, who was accompanied to the meeting by the Kazakh ambassador to the United States. The KNB's objective was to establish an agreement between the KNB and the FBI in which the FBI would assume the role of the KNB's principal partner in gathering intelligence and jointly addressing terrorism issues in Kazakhstan. Had this unlikely arrangement come to fruition, I would have had the landmine-laden job of being point man for this unusual FBI/KNB relationship—a foreign intelligence role outside the FBI's wheelhouse, which would have impaired the US government's ability to carry out its primary intelligence mission in Kazakhstan. In retrospect, it was obvious that Dutbayev's proposal was little more than a ham-handed power play, based on some sort of grievance with the US. But at that time, the proposal put me in an awkward position since I would soon be focused on building my most important relationships in Almaty. For all these reasons, accepting Dutbayev's proposal was simply not in the cards.[1]

To more fully appreciate the reasons for not agreeing to such a proposal, one should note some basic distinctions between the missions of the FBI and the CIA.

The FBI is primarily a domestic law enforcement and national security agency that is empowered to conduct criminal, counterterrorism, and counterintelligence investigations on United States territory and make arrests for violations of US law. Its primary mission includes protecting the American people against terrorist attacks, weapons of mass destruction, espionage, cyber threats, and investigating a broad range of other federal crimes and, in so doing, upholding the US Constitution. Included in the FBI's national security mission is protecting US secrets and critical assets, part of which involves monitoring and tracking suspected intelligence officers (spies) from hostile countries who are operating on US soil. But the FBI is not a foreign intelligence collection agency, and therefore, Dutbayev's attempt to maneuver the FBI into that position was not an option.

The CIA, on the other hand, is a foreign intelligence collection agency, and as such, it is restricted in its ability to gather intelligence on US persons. Its mission entails collecting and analyzing foreign intelligence that is vital to forming US policy. In so doing, the CIA collects intelligence and, in some cases, conducts covert operations on foreign soil to preempt threats against the US and strengthen US national security. Since both agencies are members of the US Intelligence Community, the director of national intelligence (DNI) oversees both agencies' intelligence activities, although the FBI is part of the Department of Justice.

In practice, the FBI and the CIA sometimes share the same contacts with host-country intelligence and law enforcement counterparts, although the nature of the relationship and the mission of each are quite different. The FBI's foreign liaison role is largely overt and is based on mutual cooperation, as both the FBI and its foreign counterparts seek to gather information and evidence from each other in support of overlapping criminal and/or terrorism investigations. Imagine a cybercriminal based in Kazakhstan who is hacking into US-based businesses. In such a case, US-based FBI agents investigating that violation of US law must rely on the legat's foreign partners to gather Kazakhstan-based evidence of that crime—partners who then share that information with US-based FBI agents through the legat. Depending on circumstances the CIA may have both a cooperative and an adversarial relationship with host-country officials. On the one hand, the CIA may work overtly with its foreign intelligence counterparts and share information as necessary to accomplish its mission of protecting US national security. In some situations it may also conduct covert operations on foreign soil in that same effort, contrary to the interests of the host government.

With my orientation and my "baptism by fire" introduction to KNB Chairman Dutbayev behind me, it was time to set out on my new adventure.

The day of my departure, Saturday, November 1, 2003, was sunny and crisp, a great day for a morning run near San Francisco's magnificent Golden Gate Bridge—the bridge I had crossed almost every day for twelve years to and from the Federal Building. It was truly the most beautiful commute imaginable, with its gently winding highway that gradually slopes downward from the north, flanked on one side by views of sun-drenched sailboats and, on the other, by mountains that extend to the ocean. On bright, blue-sky mornings, from the hills overlooking the bridge, commuters are sometimes treated to the sight of the Golden Gate towers barely peeking through a thick layer of low-lying, blinding-white fog that blankets all of downtown San Francisco. For me, in either direction, the Golden Gate was my comfort zone: the start of an interesting day at work or "Miller time"—time to decompress.

"What the **** was I thinking!" were my exact thoughts forty-eight hours later as I landed in Almaty, Kazakhstan, where it was dark, cold, and rainy; the same late fall weather I knew so well from Chicago. The next morning, I woke up in my very large, very modern Almaty apartment, big enough for a family of six. But I was a family of one—a shell-shocked, jet-lagged, and worn-out one after a thirty-two-hour trip to an outpost one FBI friend compared to a setting from the movie Dances with Wolves. Fourteen time zones from San Francisco, Almaty may as well have been a million miles from home.

The next morning, from the window of my new apartment, I could see and smell the pollution that visibly hung low to the ground when people in surrounding villages burned coal to heat their homes. And I could see the choking traffic, potholes, and the broken sidewalks outside my building. It was depressing, to say the least. These, of course, were only my initial impressions, the ones that knocked me totally off balance. And this was only the first day of my two-year commitment as legat, where I was a lone agent with my nearest FBI "neighbor" being the legat in Islamabad, Pakistan. In theory, this was the beginning of a great adventure, but that morning, I felt much as I had while staring down my first (and only) solo parachute jump—legs dangling out the door, eyes fixated three thousand feet below, and scared stiff—the last leg of a one-way trip and too late to turn back. I was clearly not in Kansas anymore, with no heels to click, no wizard to float me out, and no parachute. I thought my tour in Moscow five years earlier would have prepared me for this. So far, it had not.

With no other agent for hundreds of miles, I was cut off from my FBI family. Although the work was challenging, I would soon figure out how to get the job done. The real test was the isolation, which was complicated by the fact that I had only rare and superficial telephone contact with my supervisors at FBIHQ's Office of International Operations. I was also stripped of that false sense of security to which an agent grows accustomed after years of carrying a weapon every day, everywhere. Now my only shield was my diplomatic passport. But despite my initial misgivings, I would eventually adapt and learn to appreciate the new world I had earlier chosen as a path back to Moscow, the memory of which had remained with me since my first trip there in 1998.

When I arrived in Kazakhstan, it had been twelve years since the Soviet Union split into fifteen separate republics. But I was soon to discover that each of the Central Asian republics still shared a common language and, to an extent, a similar culture with Russians. Each country included a minority Russian population, some whose ancestors were sent to the distant republics to assert Moscow's control over governance; others who were sent to support the Soviet Union's first Five-Year Plan and the region's need for construction, manufacturing, mining, and agricultural laborers; and yet others whose ancestors were banished by Stalin to die in the wilderness. In 2003 remnants of Russian influence were predominant in a world where, during Soviet times, following a path built on Russian culture and language was how most people survived. Yet despite those similarities, each republic was unique in its history, ethnic background, culture, and mix of natural resources that sustained their economies.

In 2003 each of the five Central Asian republics was headed by an autocratic leader who rose to power during Soviet times through the ranks of the Communist Party. After assuming leadership of their newly sovereign states, those heads of state asserted Soviet-style dominance over the citizenry as they faced potential uprisings. In some cases their opposition was composed of Islamic extremists from impoverished communities, where broad disparities in wealth and power were a breeding ground for resentment and dissent. In other cases threats to Central Asian leaders were born of citizens' earnest desire to establish legitimate democracies. In response Central Asia's autocratic leaders used the police, intelligence agencies, the legislature, the courts, and control of the media to crack down on dissent. As for Western standards of democracy, such did not exist in Central Asia, where leaders were heavy-handed and corrupt, with reputations for human rights abuses, rigged elections, and repression. That was particularly true in Uzbekistan, home to violent Islamic extremists, and Tajikistan, which, six years earlier, had been in the throes of a violent civil war. In some cases Central Asian societies were built around a cult of personality in which the citizenry was reputed to have a level of adoration for their leaders that was no doubt a state-controlled, media-generated illusion. That was especially true in Turkmenistan, where the president had a godlike persona. In each country there were regions of decay left over from Soviet economies, where anything resembling Western decadence was once taboo. And all too often, there was a "me first" attitude among strangers and a general disregard for the safety of fellow citizens, just as in Moscow. See figure 6.1.

KAZAKHSTAN

Kazakhstan is bounded by Russia, China, Kyrgyzstan, Turkmenistan, and Uzbekistan. Although it is the ninth largest country in the world, I suspect few Americans (including me) learned as students where to find it on a map. Most of its population is ethnic Kazakh, and, like other Central Asian ethnicities, many are descendants of Genghiz Kahn, founder of the Mongol Empire, and the Golden Horde that dominated much of the region (including Russia) from approximately 1240–1502. Larger cities are also home to a sizeable population of ethnic Russians, and although both Russian and Kazakh languages were, and still are spoken throughout the country, Russian was the official government language in the early 2000s. Many ethnic Kazakhs' roots are in rural villages, but a

Figure 6.1. Map of the Caucasus and Central Asia.
SOURCE: WIKIMEDIA COMMONS

large percentage of their earlier ancestors lived a nomadic lifestyle until forced by Soviet leadership to work on collective farms in the 1930s—an economic upheaval that resulted in widespread famine. Like all former Central Asian republics, Kazakhstan declared its independence after the collapse of the Soviet Union. The US was the first to officially recognize Kazakhstan's independence, and to honor its early recognition, license plates of all US diplomatic vehicles prominently featured the number "1." But despite its Western-friendly orientation, Kazakhstan has traditionally maintained a carefully crafted balance between the West and its former Soviet mentors in Moscow.

Kazakhstan's best-known cities are Almaty and Astana, the latter having been renamed Nur Sultan in 2019 in honor of Nursultan Nazarbayev, Kazakhstan's first (and now former) president. Located in southeast Kazakhstan, Almaty is not far from the Chinese and Kyrgyz borders. It is Kazakhstan's largest city and its financial center and, until 1997, was the nation's capital. Almaty was also home to the US Embassy until 2006, when the embassy moved to Astana. In the early 2000s, as now, Astana was the seat of Kazakh government. Built largely after the collapse of the Soviet Union with profits from Kazakhstan's booming oil industry, Astana is the home of Kazakhstan's powerful intelligence and law enforcement agencies, which, in 2003, included the headquarters of KNB chairman Nartai Dutbayev.

Kazakhstan has several regions that are notable for their interest on the world stage. The Tengiz oil field, located near the Caspian Sea in western Kazakhstan, was discovered in 1979. The region's rich oil reserves thereafter caught the interest of major oil companies, including Chevron, Texaco, and ExxonMobile. In 1993 these and other companies entered into a forty-year joint venture known as Tengizchevroil to extract Kazakhstan's oil—all under the watchful eye of President Nazarbayev. In addition to oil, Kazakhstan is one of the largest uranium producers in the world.

The Baikonur Cosmodrome, the world's largest space launch site, is located on the flat, grassy steppes of southern Kazakhstan. Built in the 1950s, Baikonur was the beating heart of the Soviet Union's space program, having served as the 1957 launch site for Sputnik 1 (the first satellite to orbit earth) and the 1961 launch of Vostok 1, which carried Yuri Gagarin, the first man in space.[2] In 1986 Baikonur was the site from which the Soviet research space station Mir was launched, and for fifteen years, it remained international scientists' springboard to and from Mir. Over the years the Baikonur Cosmodrome remained the site from which Russian and American astronauts were launched to the International Space Station.

Semipalatinsk, located on the steppes of northeast Kazakhstan, was the Soviet Union's designated nuclear test site. From 1949 to 1989, the Soviet Union conducted hundreds of nuclear tests at Semipalatinsk, often to the peril of the nearby Kazakh population and environment. Semipalatinsk was closed in 1991, and in 1995, Kazakhstan transferred all the nuclear weapons on its territory to Russia. From 1995 to 2001, the US assisted Kazakhstan in sealing tunnels and related structures at Semipalatinsk. In 2006 Semipalatinsk became the site of the signing of the Central Asian Nuclear-Weapon-Free Zone treaty.

I had two offices in Almaty, the less secure of which was colocated with one of Kazakhstan's most successful banks. (Years later, that bank would become the focal point of an alleged multibillion-dollar-fraud scheme.[3]) The office served as a base for conducting administrative tasks and preparing unclassified documents. My other office was in the US Embassy, a tired old building, slightly offset from Almaty's main thoroughfare. The embassy was protected by a contingent of US Marine Security Guards, local Kazakh police officers, and bomb-search checkpoints at every access point. Security measures also included twenty-four-hour counter surveillance to detect potential attacks on the building. The legat office was a closet-size, windowless basement room big enough for two people, where classified documents and equipment were stored. Every day, pieces of crumbling plaster fell to the floor inside the legat office. To say the office space was depressing is an understatement, but it was my "cone of silence."

In Kazakhstan, as in the other four Central Asian countries, my host-country contacts included intelligence officials, high-ranking MVD officers, prosecutors, and officers of the tax police. In each case my mission was much like my role in Moscow: be a conduit for requests regarding criminal and terrorism matters from FBI field offices to host country law enforcement agencies, as well as for similar requests from host-country agencies to the FBI. In reviewing host-country requests, it was my duty to evaluate the nature of the request, to ensure it was not a subterfuge to gather sensitive intelligence or information that might be used for political purposes. In descending order of importance to my mission, my Kazakhstan liaison counterparts were as follows:

Committee for National Security (KNB): With responsibilities much like those of the FBI, the KNB was charged with investigating sophisticated domestic criminal and terrorist organizations. The KNB also conducted counterintelligence operations within Kazakhstan's borders and, like the CIA, was responsible for gathering intelligence outside its borders. As a political tool of President Nazarbayev, the KNB was the most powerful of all Kazakh law enforcement and intelligence agencies.

Ministry of Internal Affairs (MVD): Unlike the KNB, the MVD was largely a uniformed service, much like US state and local police. Its responsibilities included addressing street crime, criminal investigations, drug investigations, violent disturbances, and patrolling the streets.

Prosecutor General's Office (PGO): The PGO's mission was roughly equivalent to that of the US Department of Justice, as it was responsible for prosecuting violations of Kazakh law.

Tax police: Much like the IRS, the tax police's mission was to collect taxes from Kazakh businesses and citizens. Although, in a country built on corruption, enforcement of those laws was no doubt lax for those in Nazarbayev's good graces and unforgiving for Nazarbayev's political enemies.

I was now living amid the same brand of official corruption I had been investigating from a distance in San Francisco. In 2003 Kazakhstan was rated among the most corrupt countries in the world by Transparency International, an independent, global, not-for-profit agency that, as the name implies, ranks countries based on their level of corruption. Like Pavel Lazarenko's Ukraine, Nazarbayev's Kazakhstan had its share of powerful government figures who were bilking the country of capital that flowed from the country's natural resources. In Kazakhstan's case, that resource was oil. And like Ukraine, a handful of wealthy fugitives—many former political figures—thumbed their noses at Kazakh authorities as they fled to the West with proceeds allegedly stolen from their government. And since, as in the case of the US and Russia, there was no extradition treaty between the US and Kazakhstan, there was no clear path to deport citizens of Kazakhstan who entered the US legally, despite criminal charges originating in their home country. Further complicating matters were claims by these individuals that criminal charges filed against them in Kazakhstan were political vendettas. Given Kazakhstan's low rating by Transparency International, that was not a hard sell.

Nursultan Nazarbayev was the "democratically" elected president of Kazakhstan. A former Communist Party boss during Soviet times, Nazarbayev was the country's first and only president until he voluntarily stepped down in 2019. With family control of the media, parliament, the courts, and the KNB, Nazarbayev's administration (with the support of his two billionaire daughters) had the power to neutralize and/or vanquish most political opponents. Control of Kazakhstan's rich oil reserves and the almost unlimited funds they afforded Nazarbayev were the principal sources of his power and the foundation for his emerging partnerships with large Western oil companies.

One of the central figures in the emerging partnerships between Kazakhstan and Western oil companies was an American businessman whom Nazarbayev had appointed to the position of presidential advisor, complete with a Kazakh diplomatic passport. As such this individual served as an intermediary between oil companies and the Kazakh government and was responsible for facilitating deals worth hundreds of millions of dollars. In 2003 that individual was arrested by the FBI, charged with violations of the Foreign Corrupt Practices Act. Said charges stemmed from his alleged role in an eighty-million-dollar bribery scandal known as Kazakhgate. Although not specifically named in the indictment, Nazarbayev and a former prime minister were unindicted coconspirators who were purported to have received tens of millions of dollars in bribes allegedly laundered through Swiss bank accounts.[4] Despite the allegations, Nazarbayev and his former prime minister were never charged in the US, and Nazarbayev's American "advisor" was only convicted in the US of a minor misdemeanor tax charge.

Aside from allegations of rampant corruption, Kazakhstan presented a host of other hurdles before this still-green FBI legat. But before I dig deeper into those everyday challenges, it is only fair to discuss the pleasant surprises I was soon to discover, affirming that "everything does have its own good side" (Всё имеет свою хорошую сторону).

Unlike Moscow, I never personally witnessed or heard of racist or religious persecution among Kazakhstanis. (By definition, Kazakhstanis are citizens of Kazakhstan—mostly ethnic Kazakhs who tend to be Muslim and Russians who tend to be Russian Orthodox.) I witnessed weddings between Kazakhs and Russians that were as natural as anyone might find anywhere, and to my eye, there was no stigma attached to these interracial, interreligious marriages. Was I missing something? It's quite possible. But if there was animosity between ethnic Russians and Kazakhs, I never saw it, nor did anyone let me in on what may have been an otherwise well-kept secret.

My personal interactions with ethnic Kazakhs were always comfortable, given the hospitality and generosity that was extended to me at all social functions: holiday celebrations and family gatherings. I always felt welcome and at home. As in Moscow, tables were always abundant with local delicacies, although, to be sure, some, including fermented camel milk, horse milk, and horse meat, were not to my taste. And so it was always a challenge to find creative, diplomatic strategies to pass on these offers without offending the host.

Despite their break from the Soviet Union, Kazakhstanis maintained several Soviet traditions. As in all former Soviet republics, September 1 is the first day of school for young children. It is a beautiful experience to watch young Russian and Kazakh children walking en masse to school, dressed in neatly pressed black-and-white uniforms, each carrying a bouquet of flowers to honor their teachers—a tradition built on the Soviet Union's respect for education. But it was not just children who took pride in their Soviet traditions; women in Kazakhstan routinely dressed fashionably, always seeming to take great pride in their appearance wherever they went.

Kazakhstanis adhered to other Soviet traditions, including an appreciation for the arts, especially music, dance, and politically symbolic sculptures. Other vestiges of Soviet pride could be found at sites such as the Medeu, one of the world's largest high-altitude skating rinks. Located a short drive from Almaty in the Chimbulak Mountains, the Medeu was one location where Soviet skaters trained for the Olympics. The mountains of Chimbulak are also a world-class skiing area, with breathtaking winter wonderland scenes up and down the mountainsides. Down the mountain from Chimbulak is Park Ponfilov, a beautifully wooded area with monuments to Kazakh heroes of the Great Patriotic War and a historic, well-preserved wooden Russian Orthodox church.

And let me not forget Mad Murphy's Irish Bar, not far from the US and British Embassies. To me, Mad Murphy's was Almaty's answer to *Cheers*, where everyone knew your name, spoke your language, and shared in the latest "life in Kazakhstan" survival stories. It was there that I shared my first Almaty Thanksgiving dinner with my fellow American orphans. At Mad Murphy's there was no judgment. It was a place that pretended to have American-style pizza but was appreciated for the effort. It was my first stop on Sunday mornings after a hard, healthy workout, where I cheerfully undid my efforts by bellying up to the bar for a high-cholesterol breakfast, a beer, and a smoke. Mad Murphy's was a sanctuary for Western expats who craved somewhere that reminded them of home, and for many of us, it became our home away from home. For these and other reasons, I will always have a heartfelt appreciation for those days at Mad Murphy's.

I took my first flight out of Almaty a few days after my arrival: a two-hour flight to Astana. My mission was to follow up on matters discussed during the recent meeting between Director Mueller and KNB Chairman Dutbayev—the same Dutbayev who, years later, would end up sentenced to seven years in a Kazakh prison on charges of leaking state secrets and abuse of office.[5] My early morning red-eye flight was complete with breakfast and the unmistakable scent of Kazakhstan's signature culinary offering—horse meat. Talk about an eye-opener! (I passed.) As in the case of my rocky flight, my meeting with Chairman Dutbayev also failed to go smoothly. And like the horse meat, I declined Dutbayev's proposal to position the FBI as the KNB's principal partner on internal terrorism matters in Kazakhstan. All in all, it was a rough start to my new Almaty career. To be sure, there were a lot of sides to this rough start—situations that early on became a gauntlet of daily challenges requiring numerous personal adjustments. In short, I had to figure out the drill. And therein lay the rub. Did it test my character? Did I pass the test? Did I eventually put an end to my complaining? Absolutely yes, maybe, and probably not.

As one might suspect, Kazakh culinary culture is built on meat and more meat. For someone who had not eaten a steak in seventeen years, this was no small challenge, especially since I was offered horse meat by my generous hosts at every meeting and/or special event. The Zelyoni Bazaar (Green Bazaar) was Almaty's central meat market, where one could also purchase fresh fruit, vegetables, flowers, and honey. What I respected about the bazaar was the honesty of its presentation: there was no antiseptic, see-through plastic wrapping designed to sanitize, hide the smell, and protect the delicate sensibilities of the consumer, or should I say, to put as much distance between the consumer and the raw brutality, the squeals and the suffering, that go into that plate of meat at our table.

Figure 6.2.The Green Bazaar, Almaty, Kazakhstan, 2004.
SOURCE: AUTHOR'S PERSONAL COLLECTION

There was just a parade of raw, mangled flesh—horse meat, beef, pork, and lamb—hanging at eye level on hooks, often with the severed heads nearby to close the loop as a reminder of what these sentient beings looked like before someone casually ended their lives. See figure 6.2.

Smiles on the faces of store employees were hard to find. I could never figure out why. My best guess was that capitalism, the notion of profit, and the associated benefits of attracting customers were concepts that Kazakhstanis were still absorbing. The most depressing venues were the local chain grocery stores, where no one smiled, greeted customers, or offered to bag their groceries. One local acquaintance explained it this way: grocery store owners and their employees had a sense that they were doing customers a favor by providing items for sale in a convenient setting, an attitude that stemmed from Soviet times, when finding basic items was a challenge—an inconvenience that often entailed separate, long lines to purchase each individual category of goods.

After my arrival in Kazakhstan, I was not permitted to drive for several weeks until my full diplomatic status had been established. That meant either walking or taking "gypsy cabs," a system in which would-be passengers hail random private vehicles and negotiate the price of each ride with the driver. Gypsy cabs were the principal mode of transportation for many Kazakhstanis, and in most cases, vehicles were worn out, Soviet-built Zhigulis or Ladas. As a front-seat passenger, more often than not, I found myself staring into a spider-webbed, broken windshield—a dilemma, given that drivers generally took offense at the use of seatbelts. The alternative was, of course, to walk to my destination, another dilemma with a different set of challenges—ice-covered, cracked sidewalks that remained a sheet of densely packed, slippery snow throughout the season. As a result, I tended to slip and fall on the ice at least once a day, the first such occurrence having taken place on my first morning in Almaty, moments after stepping out of my new apartment. In the days to follow, it was common for me to stop and stare at the immediate path ahead, knowing full well that there was no way I was going to get through the next ten feet without falling—an inevitability, no matter how carefully I planned my steps. And much to the amusement of nearby Kazakhstanis, I'd sometimes fall, get up, and fall again.

For me, sidewalks presented other hazards, including kiosks where cigarettes were cheap, tending toward Chinese counterfeits of US brands, which presented a steady barrage of temptations for this former smoker. If passing on temptation is a test of character, I failed miserably. Adding to my struggle was the fact that Kazakhstanis smoked everywhere: in restaurants, on the street, in bars, and during official meetings. My routine was to buy a pack of Marlboros, smoke two or three, get disgusted with myself, and throw the pack away by the end of the day. Of course, the next day, I would start the ritual all over again. But kiosks were not the only sidewalk hazards. Fueled by the frustration that comes from sitting endlessly in traffic jams, drivers in Almaty were known to skirt bottlenecks by driving on the sidewalks. And if crushed snow, kiosk temptations, and maniac drivers were not enough to wake one out of his or her sidewalk reverie, one had to remain constantly alert for aggressive stray dogs.

My first week as a driver on Almaty streets was an eye-opener of a different sort. Traffic was horrific, especially on and around central Almaty's main thoroughfare. Like Moscow, streets were chaotic as drivers flaunted traffic rules with little regard for pedestrians. My impression was that, since the ability to afford a car was new to most, many people—drivers and pedestrians alike—were still learning the rules of the road and/or how to navigate a formerly uncrowded street. Whatever the reason, it is hard to comprehend drivers stuck in traffic furiously beeping at a seriously injured pedestrian lying in the middle of a busy street. Another curiosity I found were cars with small decals on the rear windshield depicting a single high-heel shoe. A local acquaintance explained that such decals were often displayed by women drivers to signal that there was a female behind the wheel—a warning of sorts, clearly stigmatizing the driver as someone whose driving ability was in question.

Overseeing the chaos on the roads were officers of the GAI (the State Automobile Inspectorate)—Kazakhstan's answer to traffic cops. Unlike the US, the GAI did not patrol the streets in vehicles and were instead positioned along the roadways on foot. They were recognizable by their unique uniforms, their large military-style hats and their *pozhaluista* ("please") sticks—bright orange sticks used to wave drivers to the side of the road, where they answered for their improper driving habits. Whether officially empowered to do so or not, the GAI tended to impose small cash "fines" on the spot, which of course was often a semitransparent means of soliciting a bribe. For drivers, fines were the cost of doing business, a form of confession that cleansed their conscience and left them free to sin again at little cost.

I learned a lot about Kazakh culture in a way I never expected, having picked up a stubborn bug during a trip to Tajikistan that caused a loss of appetite and constant coughing. As such, I was a magnet for sincere concern from local Kazakhstanis wherever I went, the silver lining having been the cures I learned from those driven to spare me my suffering. Although the remedies varied, each tended to share four common elements: vodka, garlic, butter, and mustard. Having been fully briefed on the cures, it was time to discuss the cause. Could it be germs, bacteria, or viruses? Not necessarily. The number one demon was anything cold. My dear Russian tutor, a woman of great intelligence, kindness, and talent, was convinced that the cause of my illness was eating too much ice cream, not to mention drinking cold beer and ice water. And what were the other demons? Air conditioners and fans. As I was soon to discover, not only was everything cold "bad," but anything warm or hot was "good." *Banyas* (hot saunas) were therefore a cure for everything, and if the banya was impractical, soaking one's elbows in a tub of hot water was the next best thing. When I asked why, the response was "because it's hot." When I asked why heat was healthy, the reply was "because it's not cold." And so it went. As I was to discover, there were variations on a theme. To get rid of my cough, I was told to rub vodka on my chest at night, but adding garlic and/or butter to the mix was another option. But my all-time favorite was sleeping with mustard patches on my chest. That seemed like something worth trying until I woke up not only with the same cough but a chest full of red burns. Looking back, when all was said and done, I should have realized that in a country short on modern medicine, people just do the best with what they've got.

Personal safety was always in the back of our minds in Almaty. It had only been two years since 9/11, and bomb threats were a daily reality. High-end hotels that catered to Westerners often had metal detectors positioned at their entrances, and every trip to the embassy involved thorough bomb checks under our vehicles. At one point, following threats against other regional US Embassies, the base of the embassy in Almaty was fortified with sandbags ten feet high. This was definitely getting real. But sometimes, even the simplest acts could present unique dangers, including the "door to nowhere."

It was a simple everyday visit one makes to the home of a friend. A few days before Christmas, I went to the home of an embassy coworker to deliver a small gift. She lived in a modern apartment, several stories high, that I had never before visited. After saying goodnight, I took the elevator down to the first floor. But I was soon to be harshly reminded that the "first" floor does not mean the same thing as it does in the US. In Kazakhstan the "first" floor is actually one level above the ground floor. After exiting the elevator, I walked toward what I believed to have been the same door I used to enter the building. It was not so. After opening the door, I stepped out and promptly fell twelve feet onto a snowbank. That was *not* what I was expecting! So imagine: a door that is unlocked, unmarked, serves no apparent purpose, and yes, goes nowhere. Go figure! But in hindsight, it struck me that the "door to nowhere" may have been yet another apt metaphor for former Soviets' day-to-day challenges under communism.

"To visit is good; to be home is better" (В гостях хорошо, а дома лучше) . . . It was ten months before I made my first trip back to the US. For me, this was an intensely emotional journey, an opportunity to see my dearly missed friends and return to a world where people followed a set of rules I understood. It was where I could let my guard down and where I could find the comfort food I missed, as I navigated restaurant menus that didn't need to be decoded. As I passed through US Customs, I held up the United States passport that now had a far deeper meaning than it had ten months earlier. Having seen how long it had been since I was in the US, the customs officer waved me through with a sincere "welcome home." I choked up uncontrollably, realizing how much those simple words captured a newly discovered appreciation for the country, values, people, and culture that I'd missed so much. But my return home also reminded me of another aspect of life that I sorely missed—privacy.

I have heard it said that the true test of one's character is what they do when no one is looking. One might think that, since Kazakhstan was a million miles from home, I might get a chance to test that theory. Not a chance. I was living in a fishbowl that is the US Embassy community, where everyone knew everyone else and their business. And if that didn't put enough of a dent in my privacy, I found myself reporting aspects of my personal life on paper to FBIHQ and the embassy's regional security officer, under the belief that transparency was the best way to preempt future questions. When all was said and done, my life was an open book, and I found living under a microscope exhausting.

As I delved into my new life in Kazakhstan, my monthly routine involved planning meetings not only in my new home country but also in each of the other four Central Asian republics. My mission in each country was slightly different, with some having more relevance to FBI interests than others. Of considerable interest to the FBI was my home base (Kazakhstan), where criminal matters were my primary focus, followed by Uzbekistan, where my mission was largely focused on terrorism. On the other end of the spectrum were Tajikistan, Kyrgyzstan, and Turkmenistan, where I had very few investigative leads to address. But regardless of the level of official requests for assistance, I traveled throughout Central Asia to "show the flag," to keep my developing contacts intact, and to remind embassy personnel that in case of an attack on any US Embassy, the FBI had primary jurisdiction to investigate such as a violation of US law.

Each US Embassy is its own fiefdom with its own personality. At the head of each embassy is the ambassador, the undisputed boss. Included among US ambassadors dispatched throughout the world are political appointees, who, in some cases, may require detailed briefings to acquaint them with the many complex issues associated with their appointment. In Central Asia I felt fortunate in that every ambassador to whom I reported was a career foreign service officer, steeped in an appreciation for and understanding of the State Department's multifaceted mission. For me, that meant that each ambassador was familiar with the role of the legat office and how we fit into that mission. It was therefore no surprise to me that at each post, the ambassador to whom I reported had an in-depth understanding of their country of assignment, including a deep appreciation for regional history and issues of concern to the US. And in each case, their State Department staff, including the deputy chief of mission (DCM), department heads, and locally hired foreign service nationals (FSNs), were equally professional.[6]

As is the practice, every ambassador held weekly country team meetings: confidential roundtable discussions among the American heads of each department responsible for a particular area of interest to the US. Depending on the country, sections might include economic, political, consular, public affairs, energy, and the regional security officer (RSO), plus intelligence agencies, the US Agency for International Development, and attachés from the Department of Defense, Department of Justice, FBI, DEA, and Homeland Security. Those meetings were an opportunity to brief the US ambassador and section heads on sensitive matters developing in the host country and strategies to address such issues.

Upon my arrival in each country, my first job was to introduce myself to the ambassador, with whom I reviewed the purpose of my trip and the general nature of the cases that I planned to address with host-country officials. My next meetings were with American-citizen embassy staff, who sometimes presented me with unique challenges. Among those challenges was the need to remain sensitive to what some embassy employees considered their exclusive territory as they assisted me in identifying and securing access to logical host-country contacts. At times sensitivities over territory led to the unrealistic expectation on the part of embassy staff that they would be included in my meetings with host-country officials, where confidential, law-enforcement-sensitive matters were to be discussed. And as I sorted out my working relationships with embassy personnel, I also had to decode the complex interplay among them: who was who and who was not who they claimed to be. That, too, could be a challenge, as the official positions of some American-citizen embassy employees disguised their true roles as undeclared intelligence officers.

UZBEKISTAN

Uzbekistan is a poor country with a largely Muslim population, which is bordered by Afghanistan, Tajikistan, Kyrgyzstan, Turkmenistan, and Kazakhstan. Its historic claim to fame is its place on the Silk Road, the two-thousand-year-old, four-thousand-mile textile trade route that linked East Asia with ancient Persia, the Arabian Peninsula, East Africa, and Southern Europe. Popular tourist sites along the Silk Road include Uzbek cities known for their centuries-old mosques: Bukhara and Samarkand, the latter being the burial site of the fourteenth-century Mongol conqueror Timur, founder of the Timurid Empire. But for me, Uzbekistan's once notable place in world history was a distant memory in the early 2000s, as its economy struggled, given its adherence to a Soviet-style command economy that did little to attract Western investment and economic development. As a result, Uzbekistan was far less prosperous than its oil-rich, Western-friendly neighbor to the north

(Kazakhstan). The resulting poverty and low wages helped set the stage for devastating political unrest.

In the turbulent days of the late 1990s / early 2000s, Uzbekistan was a breeding ground for terrorism. The Islamic Movement of Uzbekistan (IMU), a group composed of Al-Qaeda-linked Islamic extremists, was active in the region, with bases in neighboring Tajikistan and Afghanistan. Although the movement suffered severe losses in battles against US-led forces in Afghanistan, the IMU's principal enemy was Uzbekistan's ruthless president, Islam Karimov, whom the IMU hoped to overthrow and replace with a government based on Sharia law. Their hatred of Karimov stemmed from his willingness to allow US access to an Uzbek airbase in support of the war in Afghanistan and his brutal suppression of domestic political uprisings. One gruesome form of torture credibly attributed to Karimov was the practice of forcing persons under interrogation into tubs of hot water, gradually boiling them alive if they refused to cooperate. Uzbekistan's struggle with violent extremism and its proximity to Afghanistan, where the war against Al-Qaeda was raging, were factors in my decision to travel to Uzbekistan soon after my arrival in Central Asia. In the months to come, I took the two-hour flight from Almaty to Tashkent, Uzbekistan's seat of government, nearly every month.

Since I was without a vehicle in Tashkent, I generally took public transportation from my hotel to the embassy. I was impressed by the respect I was given, which was likely due to my suit and gray hair. Teenagers routinely offered their seats, and I had the impression that Uzbek citizens had a favorable attitude toward Americans. The uniformed MVD officers who patrolled the streets and subways were another story. They were poorly paid and had a reputation for corruption, known to wear their uniforms on their days off as they solicited bribes from the citizenry. As a Westerner, I was an obvious target, and MVD officers occasionally tried to shake me down on the metro. That is when a diplomatic passport came in handy, and whenever I had to show my passport, I always added, in a sharply spoken reminder, "Diplomat!"—an announcement that put an end to the conversation.

One popular Tashkent attraction was the Chorsu Market, an indoor/outdoor market very much like Almaty's Green Bazaar. The market was a place I regularly frequented in my off-hours, that is, until April 2004, when terrorists launched a suicide bombing at the market that coincided with attacks against Tashkent-based police officers. Tension was definitely in the air, and each of my walks from the Tashkent metro to the US Embassy was unnerving. Like my embassy colleagues, I was in a state of heightened awareness, scrutinizing every person and every vehicle each time I approached the entrance to the embassy, always with a tight knot in my stomach.

The US Embassy consisted of an aging building complex set approximately twenty feet from a tree-lined street. The main employee entrance to the embassy was off a sidewalk that ran parallel to the street. Within fifty feet, also on that sidewalk, was the consular office's walk-up window, where Uzbek citizens submitted applications for US visas. Although it was guarded by a handful of uniformed Uzbek MVD officers, the US Embassy in Tashkent did not have a detachment of US Marine Security Guards. The reason? According to my understanding, a US Embassy had to be structurally defensible to qualify for an MSG detail. Catch-22.

When America was attacked on September 11 less than three years earlier, I had been on the opposite side of the country, far from harm's way. Like most of my FBI coworkers, I was part of the mad scramble for information that was everyone's focus. And for those New Yorkers, passengers and crew of four ill-fated flights bound for California, Pentagon employees, first responders, and survivors who continue to suffer long after, it is, of course, impossible to imagine any horror comparable to the attacks of that day. But for those affiliated with the US Embassy in Uzbekistan in July 2004, Tashkent was where the rubber met the road and the excrement hit the fan once again. As if anyone needed a reminder of the target on Americans' backs, a suicide bombing at the embassy a week after my return from a routine trip to Tashkent got my full attention, as it did for the far more vulnerable employees who reported to the embassy every morning: foreign service officers, attachés, foreign service nationals, and MVD officers, whose job it was to guard the embassy's vulnerable exterior. All this talk about terrorism was for real. The madness was for real. The attack was for real.

The embassy bombing took place on July 30, 2004, late on a Friday afternoon. At the moment of the bombing, I was in Almaty, when, one hour later, I was informed of the attack by my FBI supervisor in Washington, who directed me to return to Tashkent the following morning to assume control of the crime scene and preserve evidence of this crime against the United States.[7] Tashkent by the next morning? Good luck with that! It generally took me two weeks in advance to reserve a seat on Uzbek Air, and an unpredictable ten-hour overnight drive on unfamiliar, treacherous mountain roads was not an option. Months of frustration exploded in one conversation, and I knew my superiors at FBIHQ had little concept of the idiosyncrasies that defined day-to-day life in Central Asia. But with a little help from my friends, I was able to get to Tashkent by eight thirty the next morning. And who were my heroes? They were the Almaty-based US government officials who mentored me starting on day one of my arrival in Central Asia.

Early the next morning, I was the sole passenger on a twin-engine prop plane en route to Tashkent. Once I arrived on the scene, evidence of the attack's brutal destruction was everywhere. Although the remains of the bomber's dismembered torso had been removed, pieces of his flesh were splattered on the embassy walls, sidewalk, and nearby tree trunks. (One bit of trivia I learned is that bees are attracted to rotting human flesh, thus, the clusters of bees all around the blast site.) The heart of the explosion was the shattered consular office window, where the bomber had detonated his bomb-laden briefcase. Also at the scene were patches of dried blood, where two MVD officers had been killed by the blast while protecting American citizens.

It soon became clear that the bombing was one of three simultaneous, coordinated attacks, minutes apart, by persons who were later determined to be Al-Qaeda-trained terrorists. Within minutes of the bombing at the US Embassy, the nearby Israeli Embassy and the Uzbek prosecutor general's office (PGO) were similarly attacked.[8] In addition to the two MVD officers killed at the US Embassy, two Uzbek guards, including the Israeli ambassador's personal bodyguard, were killed at the

Israeli Embassy. At the American Embassy, the bomber barely missed his chance to get inside the embassy's vulnerable interior and murder countless Americans, having failed in his attempt to grab the normally locked entrance door as those employees entered and exited the building. What was plan B? The bomber placed his briefcase in front of the consular office window, which was accessible from the public sidewalk. The blast blew out the window, with deadly shrapnel barely missing the two foreign service nationals whose job was to process US visa applications.

My immediate objective was to preserve the crime scene and, as quickly as possible, get FBI evidence technicians on the scene to sift through the evidence and ensure a proper chain of custody. And although there were several bits of evidence scattered on the sidewalk and street, I was certainly no expert on the intricate procedures for handling a bomb scene. But I was in luck. Two FBI evidence technicians who had long before applied for and obtained valid visas to enter Uzbekistan on an unrelated matter were on site the next day. In the meantime a pair of Israeli bomb experts who had responded to the bombing at the Israeli Embassy provided me with enough expertise to keep me afloat.

Apart from physical evidence, there were several pieces of the puzzle yet to uncover. Who organized the attacks? Who funded the attacks? Did the IMU play a role? But the most critical question of all was whether there were plans in the works for follow-up attacks. Answers to all of those questions were essential, and decisions had to be prioritized, balancing both the need to head off a possible second strike and the desire to successfully prosecute the accused in US court. So began the strategizing, and although prevention and prosecution were not mutually exclusive, it was clear that the immediate priority was determining whether there were plans in the works for future bombings.

As we sought answers to these questions, several strategic considerations had to be taken into account, not the least of which was whether Uzbek authorities would simply step aside and allow the FBI to assume full control of a massive criminal investigation on their home turf. Had the Uzbeks declined to step aside in favor of the FBI, successful prosecution in the US would have hinged on the alternative—trusting Uzbek authorities to conduct a professional investigation that conformed to the rigorous legal standards demanded by a US court, and whether they would be willing to extradite their own citizens to the US for trial. Given the two alternatives, the only reasonable path to a successful criminal prosecution in US court would have been a thorough investigation by the FBI on Uzbek soil.

But preventing a follow-up attack meant moving fast, an approach that, under the circumstances, was viewed by those of us on the ground as incompatible with a painstaking investigative process and a successful US prosecution. In cases where the FBI is thrust into an investigation outside its traditional boundaries on short notice, moving fast is easier said than done. It takes time to negotiate host-country approval for a small army of FBI personnel to investigate on foreign soil, to process visa applications allowing FBI agents with official passports to enter the country, to organize and vet qualified linguists, and to lay the ground rules with local law enforcement authorities for an investigation that will pass muster in US court (e.g., no Uzbek "polygraphs" or hot tub confessions). It takes time to ship evidence to the FBI lab for analysis and to explain Fifth Amendment rights and the right to an attorney to non-American suspects. If attorneys get involved, that's another speed bump. To have prevented another attack, speed was essential, and moving too slowly would have given those responsible time to regroup and strike again.

In the best-case scenario, assuming suspects would one day be identified and arrested, the lack of an extradition treaty between the US and Uzbekistan posed another dilemma: how to legally transfer arrestees into US custody. If subjects somehow ended up in the US, we would have had to plan for another possibility—a dismissal in US court or the outside chance that the accused might be found not guilty by a US jury. Having seen this movie in San Francisco, I knew that deporting foreign nationals after an acquittal is not as easy as it appears. Individuals in such cases typically claim asylum, and in our subjects' case, that would have been an easy sell, given Uzbek President Karimov's reputation for extreme brutality. So what normally happens under such circumstances? Foreign citizens acquitted of serious crimes in the US remain in the US while their asylum case is under consideration, with little threat of incarceration.

In short, although we preferred to see the guilty parties land in US prison, I agreed with my intelligence counterparts that prioritizing prosecution in the US risked leaving open a window of opportunity for violent extremists to pull off a follow-up attack. The remaining path therefore centered on finding what Russians refer to as the "golden middle" (Золотая середина), a middle ground where both objectives—prevention and prosecution—could be satisfied. That golden middle turned out to be a compromise: put the FBI in the passenger's seat while Central Asian authorities, supported by their American counterparts, gathered intelligence. And should the subjects be identified and arrested, we would then be in a position to present FBI lab analysis, physical evidence, bomb-tech expertise, and expert testimony in a Central Asian court. As the situation progressed, my decision put me squarely at odds with my respected fellow agents in the FBI's Washington field office.

In the weeks to follow, Uzbek and Kazakh authorities identified a man believed to have been a principal organizer of the bombings. Kazakh KNB officers subsequently captured him trying to escape Uzbekistan through a city on the Kazakh border, where he was charged under Kazakh law with activities associated with his membership in a terrorist organization. I later observed his KNB interrogation through a live video feed at a KNB office in Almaty, during which I witnessed no irregularities. In the end he admitted to his role as an organizer of the attacks, his affiliation with a group of Al-Qaeda-linked terrorists, and the fact that he had been trained by Al-Qaeda in Pakistan.[9] And although the core of the crime had taken place in Uzbekistan, Kazakhstan's more powerful and influential authorities prosecuted him and his fellow conspirators on terrorism charges in Kazakhstan. At that point it was time for my first experience in a Kazakh court of law.

Over my career I had testified in court countless times. I felt comfortable in court, and as my career progressed, I came to enjoy the toe-to-toe wrangling with defense attorneys. US federal courts are where all constitutional rights are carefully explained to defendants and where defendants are afforded a clear presumption of innocence and legal representation. In federal courts judges demand strict adherence to Federal Rules of Criminal Procedure and Federal Rules of Evidence, thus giving the proceedings an air of fairness and a sense of reverence for the US Constitution. Federal courts are places where facts are proven by carefully scrutinized evidence and where determining truth is the ultimate goal. But the trial I was about to witness was like nothing I had ever experienced. This was a whole new way of dealing with criminal suspects—a remnant of the old Soviet system in which there was no right to a jury and where there was a clear, if unspoken, presumption of guilt.

Several weeks after the arrest of the subjects, two young FBI bomb experts, a Kazakhstani attorney, and I flew from Almaty to Shymkent, Kazakhstan, near the Uzbek border. From there we were escorted by a contingent of heavily armed Kazakh MVD officers, with lights and sirens all the way on the three-hour drive to Taraz, Kazakhstan, where the trial was to take place. Upon our arrival we were put up in a hotel where we were given twenty-four seven MVD escorts and protection. The MVD was taking no chances with our safety. See figure 6.3.

Figure 6.3. Kazakh MVD Protection Detail, Taraz, Kazakhstan, 2004.
SOURCE: AUTHOR'S PERSONAL COLLECTION

The trial was a foregone conclusion. Thirteen defendants sat through the ordeal, seated in a metal cage located squarely in the center of the courtroom. The cage was positioned steps away from the three ornately robed judges, who were seated several feet above eye level at a long desk that was set atop a raised platform. Attorneys called cowering witnesses, who were required to stand in front of and look upward at the judges as they testified. There was no question as to who had the power and who had none. As the trial progressed, it was obvious that the defendants would be found guilty. It was just a matter of how the prosecutors and judges would get there and how many years the defendants would spend in prison. In the end our FBI bomb tech provided expert testimony, complete with professionally prepared illustrations that described how the bomb was constructed and detonated. He was no doubt the first FBI agent to ever testify in a Kazakh court. At the conclusion of the trial, all defendants were found guilty and sentenced to prison. Were there any immediate follow-up attacks? No. And what about the golden middle? I think we found it.

Tajikistan

Tajikistan is a very poor, landlocked country, the smallest of the five Central Asian republics. It is bordered by Afghanistan, China, Uzbekistan, and Kyrgyzstan. Tajikistan's seat of government is Dushanbe, a city surrounded by mountains. A Muslim country, Tajikistan has a population that is largely composed of an ethnic Iranian group (Tajik) that speaks a Persian language similar to that spoken in Iran (Farsi). Tajik industry is based on aluminum processing and chemical production. It is also rich in minerals. But its unemployment rate is high, and many Tajiks end up as migrant workers in Russia.

At the time of my first visit to Tajikistan, the country had been six years removed from a bloody civil war that began soon after the dissolution of the Soviet Union. Tens of thousands of Tajiks were killed during that conflict, which also led to the displacement of a large portion of the country's population. The war centered on an attempt to overthrow Tajikistan's first autocratic leader, who was subsequently arrested by opposition forces at the Dushanbe airport in 1992. The civil war ended with the installment of another autocratic former Communist Party boss, Emomali Rahmon, as Tajikistan's new leader—a position he holds to this day despite an assassination attempt in 1997 and coup attempts in 1997 and 1998.

The US Embassy in Tajikistan was a run-down building with a maze of narrow hallways leading to various offices. Like the embassy in Tashkent, it did not have a contingent of US Marine Security Guards, and the building always had an air of vulnerability. After the 2004 suicide bombing at the US Embassy in neighboring Tashkent, a small makeshift guard post consisting of sandbags and armed Tajik guards was built outside the entrance to the embassy. Considering those terrifying developments, I can only imagine the anxiety of each embassy employee as he or she contemplated their daily trip to and from work. It was just one more reason I had to respect my State Department colleagues and their FSN staff.

Much like in Uzbekistan, my focus in Tajikistan was terrorism. But since there were very few ties—business, travel, or otherwise—between Tajikistan and the US, there were very few requests for assistance from FBI field offices of either a criminal or terrorist nature. That is why I traveled to Tajikistan only four times during my time in Central Asia. But when I did, I faced safety concerns much like those in Tashkent, as well as other challenges that were far more mundane.

In Dushanbe I stayed at the only hotel recommended by the US Embassy. The Avesto Hotel was a large, run-down, Soviet-era building on Dushanbe's main street. It was one of a kind. Positioned near a mosque with its minarets visible from the hotel windows, I was greeted each morning with a unique wake-up call—the very loud early morning call to prayer that served as my alarm clock. The hotel had other unique features, especially its décor, which was seemingly designed for disorientation. The carpeting on the floor was a dizzying array of patterns and colors that were in direct conflict with the equally dizzying patterns and colors on the wallpaper. Taking a shower was not possible. Baths were the only option, and I always found myself sitting atop a thin layer of mud that had settled on the base of the tub.

As I traveled throughout Dushanbe, I developed a soft spot for Tajiks, who always greeted me with a gentle hand over their heart in what struck me as a uniquely sincere gesture of warmth and respect. How could one not respond kindly to that? That soft spot also sprang from the realization that most Tajiks were severely impoverished, at the mercy of violent internal power struggles over which they had little control. For all these reasons, my exposure to Tajiks had a far greater impact on me personally than did the nature of the work, and I always appreciated the respect I was afforded by both the local population and the embassy staff.

KYRGYZSTAN

Kyrgyzstan is bordered by China, Uzbekistan, Tajikistan, and Kazakhstan. With its northern border near Almaty, it was the only Central Asian country to which I could travel by car—always with a driver who knew how to navigate the region's treacherous highways and insane drivers. Although an immediate neighbor, Kyrgyzstan was not blessed with the same natural resources that enabled Kazakhstan to prosper, and as a poor country, it, too, was a source of migrant workers for Russia. Like Kazakhs, many ethnic Kyrgyz had lived a nomadic lifestyle until the country's incorporation into the Soviet Union. To survive, most Kyrgyz raised livestock and farmed. Agriculture in this mountainous country was difficult, requiring Kyrgyzstan's investment in heavy machinery. Like those in other Central Asian countries, Kyrgyzstan's leaders were autocratic, leading to political tensions and attempts to overthrow the government. In 2005 the Tulip Revolution, fueled by charges of authoritarianism and corruption, led to the forcible removal of Kyrgyzstan's president, a development that drew the attention of autocratic leaders from other former Soviet republics, especially Russia.

As in the case of Tajikistan, I rarely had business in Bishkek (the capital of Kyrgyzstan). But like in Tajikistan, I felt a responsibility to establish an FBI presence. Having said that, I cannot recall an instance in which I either requested information from or provided information to my Kyrgyz counterparts.

TURKMENISTAN

Turkmenistan, like Tajikistan, Uzbekistan, and Kyrgyzstan, is a largely Muslim country. It is bordered by Iran, Afghanistan, Uzbekistan,

Kazakhstan, and the Caspian Sea. From the capital, Ashgabat, it is a short drive to the Iranian border. In general, I did not see many Westerners in Ashgabat. Turkmenistan was not an easy place to get a visa to enter, nor was it an easy place for its citizens to leave. Like with Uzbekistan, parts of Turkmenistan are prominently located on what was once the Silk Road. The country is largely ethnic Turkmen, although the population includes a host of other regional ethnicities. Turkmenistan is a major producer of natural gas, the foundation of its economy.

Turkmenistan was another world; a night-and-day difference between it and any other Central Asian country. In some ways, it reminded me of what it must be like to live in North Korea. In another way, it reminded me of Las Vegas. And yet Turkmenistan had the surreal feel of Disneyland.

Like in North Korea, Turkmenistan worshipped its "dear leader," a cult-like presidential figure who was known by the moniker Turkmen Bashi (Chief of the Turks). His real name was Saparnurot Niyazov, and he had held the office of president since the country gained its independence after the collapse of the Soviet Union. Turkmen Bashi's ever-present likeness was a constant reminder of his larger-than-life prominence in Turkmen society. For me, it began with the Turkmen Air flight from Almaty to Ashgabat, where his picture adorned the interior of the plane. Giant depictions of Turkmen Bashi were built into most of the modern government buildings in downtown Ashgabat, and whatever he did seemed to be newsworthy. Simply arriving at his namesake airport was a major news event, as he was greeted by a crowd of young child worshippers, who were dressed in traditional attire, singing his praises. See figure 6.4.

I could never figure out whether downtown Ashgabat reminded me more of Las Vegas or Disneyland. Everywhere in this cloudless desert environment were fountains and beautiful and modern white stone government buildings, but there was one catch: I never saw anyone entering or leaving these buildings. And I would have known. Like in my days in Washington, DC, I routinely went for jogs around downtown whenever I was in Ashgabat, a running-while-sightseeing tour of the city. Beautiful fountains, sculptures, and buildings were interspersed with oversized

Figure 6.4.Turkmen Bashi Photo on Government Building, Ashgabat, Turkmenistan, 2004.
SOURCE: AUTHOR'S PERSONAL COLLECTION

replicas of the Ruhnama (the Book of the Soul), allegedly written by Turkmen Bashi as a spiritual guide for daily life in Turkmenistan. But who were the only people I saw? The poor, aging, colorfully dressed babushkas who meticulously washed the base of the buildings' exteriors. Go figure! Like Las Vegas, Ashgabat struck me as a city where buildings pretended to be something they weren't. And like Disneyland, it appeared that downtown Ashgabat was Turkmen Bashi's personal "happy place."

Much like Ashgabat's empty downtown buildings, the newly built luxury high-rise President Hotel was a continuation of my journey into the surreal. Having checked in after midnight, I was not surprised to see an empty lobby. But what I did see was a full staff. The next morning I was the only guest in the hotel's very modern fitness center. After work I had dinner at the elegant hotel restaurant. Once again, I had it all to myself despite the restaurant being fully staffed. After dinner I went to the full-staffed bar—no one! So, like those beautiful yet empty downtown government buildings, the President Hotel, I concluded, was either built for show or was another aspect of Turkmen Bashi's "field of dreams" world—a classic case of the following: "If you build it, they will come."

As in the cases of Tajikistan and Kyrgyzstan, FBI field offices rarely sent me requests for assistance in Turkmenistan, nor do I recall ever receiving such requests from Turkmen officials. Nonetheless, an official from Turkmen Bashi's office routinely sat in on each of my meetings with Turkmen officials, diligently taking detailed notes in the process. It wasn't difficult to read the anxiety on the faces of the officials with whom I met, clearly in fear that something they might say would displease Turkmen Bashi. To say that this man's presence put a damper on candid conversations was an understatement. Fortunately, since I had little business in Turkmenistan, I paid no real price for the charade. But my State Department counterparts undoubtedly found this an obstacle to accomplishing their missions.

One curious feature of the official photos plastered everywhere in downtown Ashgabat was Turkmen Bashi's thick head of jet-black hair—not bad for a man who was born in 1940. But when God is on your side,

Figure 6.5. Tower Topped by Golden Statue of Turkmen Bashi, Ashgabat, Turkmenistan, 2004.
SOURCE: AUTHOR'S PERSONAL COLLECTION

miracles happen. And legend had it that God, in fact, magically turned Turkmen Bashi's head of thick gray hair to black. (One of my cherished keepsakes is an old watch featuring Turkmen Bashi's true gray hair.) But the doctored photos of Turkmen Bashi, prominently displayed throughout Turkmenistan, did not hold a candle to the soaring white tower located in Ashgabat's city center and topped with a golden statue of Turkmen Bashi, his arms extended as this mystical guru seemingly basked in the adoration of his imaginary worshippers. The statue itself was set atop a rotating platform, high in the air, and was programmed so that his face always pointed toward the sun. For me, this was the ludicrous last stop on a Turkmen Bashi magical mystery tour that featured one man's obsession with his appearance, his outsized sense of self-importance, and the blind devotion of his loyal followers. See figure 6.5.

As I was preparing to put Central Asia behind me, lines from familiar songs kept popping into my head. Along with a line from the Grateful Dead's "Truckin" ("what a long strange trip it's been") was an old Allan Sherman song: "Hello Mudduh, Hello Fadduh!"[10] The song is a comedic take on a small boy's first day at summer camp. It's raining. There's poison ivy and alligators. He's miserable and writes his parents a letter, begging them to take him home. He explains the reasons for his misery and tells them his tale of woe. As he continues to beg his parents to rescue him, the sun comes out, and kids start playing. After things steadily improve, he does an about-face and closes his letter by telling his parents, "Mudduh, Fadduh kindly disregard this letter." In short, maybe Central Asia wasn't so bad after all, and maybe it helped prepare me for the long, even stranger trip that was yet to come.

CHAPTER 7

Strange Bedfellows

SOURCE: СЧИТАЛОЧКА BY BORIS ZAKHODER

Once up a time there were two neighbors.	Жили-были два соседа
Two neighbors who were cannibals.	Два соседа-людоеда.
One cannibal invited the other cannibal to his home for lunch.	Людоеда Людоед
	Приглашает На обед.
The cannibal replied, "No. I will not come to your home for lunch.	Людоед ответил: Нет— Не пойду к тебе, сосед
To come for lunch is not a bad idea,	На обед попасть не худо,
But not as some kind of meal!"	Но отнюдь Не в виде Блюда!

Can two entrenched rivals comfortably coexist? In the case of the FBI and the former KGB, we were all too familiar with the deadly nature of our shared spy vs. spy history. We understood each other's motivations, strategies, and objectives. We were natural enemies, deeply familiar with a history born of mutual mistrust and animosity, each driven to infiltrate the other in the struggle to win the battle of ideas. As we shared the same space, we instinctively knew we must adhere to certain rules of engagement: never let your guard down, keep a safe distance, and sleep with one eye open. These were words to live by in Moscow, and this poem, which I learned early in my Russian language studies, would, in the summer of 2005, become a metaphor for my new role as Moscow's legal attaché.[1]

The Moscow vacancy was advertised in the spring of 2005, when I was eighteen months into my Almaty assignment. It was a door that opened every two to three years—the life span of a legat tour of duty. Once offered the position, I scheduled briefings at the State Department and CIA headquarters, much like those I had attended prior to my Almaty assignment. My meeting at the State Department's Foggy Bottom headquarters was pro forma. Since the US Embassy in Moscow was one of the most politically sensitive in the world, I assume the State Department wanted to check out the person representing FBI interests in their "house." My meeting at CIA headquarters was another matter. It was then that I realized what I was getting into, and it was clear that the spy-vs.-spy world of the mid-1980s had come full circle, that Moscow in 2005 was a far cry from Moscow in 1998, when I was first exposed to this enigmatic new world. The CIA briefed me on one Russian in particular—Alexander Zhomov—a KGB staff officer who played an integral role in the devastating blows struck against US intelligence during the Year of the Spy (1985), an era when both US and Soviet intelligence agencies were immersed in an intelligence tug-of-war—a deadly serious game of red rover that had been ongoing since before the days of Boris and Natasha in which well-placed, would-be spies were lured behind enemy lines into each other's inner sanctum.

In the mid-1980s, Zhomov was a high-ranking official in the KGB's Second Chief Directorate–American Department who was responsible for monitoring foreign citizens residing in the Soviet Union and countering US spying operations. His day job likely included oversight of physical and technical surveillance (wiretaps) of Americans working at the US Embassy in Moscow and learning everything there was to know about their private and professional lives. He was a shark in search of blood, whose ocean was the embassy compound. But an even more clandestine side of his KGB duties was developing a ruse in which he would offer his services to the CIA as a defector. In the language of spies, he was a "dangle," whom the CIA warily took under their wing and code-named Prologue.[2] In fact, he was a loyal KGB officer whose true objective was to uncover CIA secrets, including how the CIA helped KGB defectors escape from the Soviet Union to the West. During this years-long subterfuge, Zhomov also provided disinformation to the CIA that helped mask the true identities of the Soviet Union's prize double agents—CIA officer Aldrich Ames and FBI supervisor Robert Hanssen—spies who inflicted devasting blows against the United States in the 1980s and 1990s.[3] If you were then a dedicated young KGB officer, Alexander Zhomov was the kind of officer you aspired to become.

The two men whose betrayal Zhomov was tasked with concealing are considered the most successful spies in KGB history. In April 1985 Aldrich Ames, a former high-ranking figure in the CIA's Soviet counterintelligence section, volunteered his services to the Soviet *rezident*—the chief of KGB spying operations at the Soviet Embassy in Washington, DC. Did he do so out of principle? In his book *Spy Handler*, Ames's KGB handler, deputy rezident Viktor Cherkashin, claims that Ames, like most spies, was motivated not by ideology but by personal benefit. According to Cherkashin, the KGB allocated over two million dollars for payment to Ames for information including the identities of KGB defectors and other Soviet officials who were secretly providing information to the CIA and FBI—a fair sum, considering that the information provided by Ames helped torpedo CIA operations in Moscow and exposed the identities of two Washington-based KGB officers who were providing information to the FBI.[4] What fate might those defectors expect? A bullet to the back of the head in the basement of Moscow's brutal Lefortovo Prison. No public trial, no appeal. And what became of Ames? He was arrested by the FBI in 1994 on espionage charges and subsequently sentenced to life in federal prison.

But Ames was not the only high-ranking KGB spy whose identity Zhomov helped conceal. FBI supervisor Robert Hanssen, who oversaw the

FBI's intelligence budget and, later, the Soviet analytical unit at FBIHQ, offered his services to the KGB for money in October 1985. Like Ames, Hanssen exposed the identities of KGB defectors, but he also provided the Soviets with information on US spy satellites, a plan to build listening posts under the Soviet Embassy, plans to recruit KGB officers in the US, and details of the FBI's counterintelligence budget.[5] Like Ames, Hanssen's KGB handler was Viktor Cherkashin, who claims that the harm inflicted against the US by Hanssen was greater than the damage done by Ames. And like Ames, the information provided by Hanssen to the KGB is alleged to have led to the summary execution of CIA and FBI sources. Hanssen was arrested by the FBI in 2001, and from 2002 until his death in June 2023, he served fifteen consecutive life sentences at the federal supermax prison in Florence, Colorado.

As in the case of JFK's speech to the nation during the Cuban Missile Crisis and his assassination thirteen months later, I vividly recall where I was when I first learned of Hanssen's arrest. I was in my San Francisco office, wearing a Russian *shapka* (military hat), celebrating my fiftieth birthday. It was a challenging day on both counts, but my personal adjustment to the start of my sixth decade paled in comparison to the pain the organization I loved was experiencing. Hanssen's betrayal was a frontal assault on who we were—the kind of blow that bursts an FBI agent's bubble, especially for the overwhelming majority of us, who believe in our cause to our core. After years of taking immense pride in the firm belief that we were the cavalry in white hats, this was a sharp kick to that tender place that hurts the most. One veteran San Francisco agent who dedicated his entire career to intelligence battles with the Soviets (and Russians) sat down in my office that day a broken man, recounting how his life's work had suddenly gone up in smoke. Hanssen had undermined everything he'd accomplished, despite what he had once celebrated as his successes. In short, it was a bad day all around for those of us who took extreme pride in our mission, our values, and our FBI family. But my feeling of betrayal went deeper, now struck by my naïveté and the budding (now dimming) optimism I once felt after my return home from Moscow in the spring of 1998.

Not long after my CIA orientation, as I was preparing to head to Moscow, I was invited to a meeting in Washington between Director Mueller and his Russian counterpart, Nikolai Patrushev, who, six years prior, had replaced Vladimir Putin as chairman of the FSB (formerly the KGB).[6] On the FBI side of the table, Director Mueller was accompanied by FBI foreign counterintelligence experts, my Moscow predecessor, and this new kid on the block. Patrushev's delegation included FSB generals, his security team, and the US intelligence community's nemesis, Alexander Zhomov (Sasha, as he preferred to be called), whose presence, as told to me by one FBIHQ veteran, was a "sharp stick in the eye" of the FBI.[7] In short, it was clear that Patrushev's selection of Zhomov as a member of his delegation was a message—a middle finger to the FBI. Russia was back, the once-open window of the 1990s was now nailed shut, and the game was on.

Those were the challenges I faced as I set out for my new assignment in July 2005. Clearly, a lot had changed since my first assignment seven years earlier. In 2005 Moscow was one of the most expensive cities in the world, home to booming businesses and fine restaurants, which was a far cry from Moscow of 1998, when Russia was struggling with hyperinflation, chaos, and decay. In 1998 our partners were hard-working, fun-loving MVD officers, who offered plenty of extended handshakes in an atmosphere of promising beginnings, a glimmer of trust, and cautious optimism. And back then, this Cold War kid, like millions of others, was naïve enough to believe that Russia was well on the road to democracy, that the Soviet Union was lying in its coffin with a silver stake in its heart.

But by 2005, President Vladimir Vladimirovich Putin was busy sealing the cracks in the wall and mending the tear in the Iron Curtain. By that time, Putin, the magician, was well on his way to putting the democracy genie back in the bottle and the toothpaste back in the tube. His clear purpose was to revive Soviet national pride and, like in the glory days of Stalin, Khrushchev, and Yuri Andropov, reestablish the Soviet Union's position as a power player on the world stage.[8] As he did so, the FSB grew stronger, and the freedoms that Russians had gotten a taste of under Yeltsin—open elections, freedom of speech, freedom of the press, freedom of assembly, and the right to dissent (many of which were guaranteed in the 1993 Russian constitution)—were under serious threat. In the process, Putin had begun rebuilding the FSB into Russia's most formidable law enforcement, counterintelligence, and domestic security agency, which, like in the glory days of the KGB, was becoming a heavy-metal boot on the neck of political dissent. In short, Moscow in 2005 was a whole new ballgame. This time there would be no clowning. The FBI's principal partner was now the FSB, which was unquestionably Russia's big dog and the undisputed leader of the Russian pack. And although our mission was much like that of my first Moscow tour, the game was being played under drastically different rules—all business— each cannibal wary of being eaten by the other. What was the bottom line? It was time to learn the new rules, one of which stemmed from a built-in contradiction within the FSB's mission: On the one hand, in the spirit of cooperation, our FSB partners worked with the legat staff to find our golden middle by carving out a narrow range of mutual interests; some focused on overlapping criminal cases, many centered on terrorism. On the other hand, we knew that our partners' colleagues in the counter-intelligence wing of the FSB were equally intent on recruiting spies from within the US intelligence community. That, of course, would include the legat staff.

In descending order of importance to the FBI's mission and overall power in the Russian law enforcement and intelligence structure, the following were our host-country counterparts:

Federal Security Service (FSB): The FSB grew out of Mikhail Gorbachev's decision to disband the KGB in 1991. The present-day FSB was officially established in 1995, following reorganization of a similarly titled agency that, upon dissolution of the Soviet Union, was created to replace the domestic counterintelligence branch of the KGB. In the years I worked in Russia (2005–2007), the FSB was charged with investigating sophisticated criminal and terrorist organizations and countering foreign intelligence operations on Russian soil (which included recruiting foreign spies). Under Putin the FSB gradually expanded its former KGB domestic security role of monitoring Russian citizens and crushing political dissent. The FSB had an international department that coordinated with foreign law enforcement and intelligence agencies on matters of mutual interest: terrorism, organized crime, cybercrime, and financial investigations. The FSB also had an elite Special Weapons and Tactics (SWAT) team (Alpha Team), a paramilitary organization responsible for addressing violent domestic crises. In the mid-2000s, Lubyanka, which in the past had served as the headquarters of the NKVD and KGB, still served as headquarters for branches of the FSB. The chairman of the FSB was (and still is) appointed by and directly answers to the president of the Russian Federation.[9]

Foreign Intelligence Service (SVR): Like the FSB, the SVR emerged from Gorbachev's decision to disband the KGB in 1991. At that time, the SVR continued the KGB's foreign intelligence and espionage missions, which, under the KGB, were part of the prestigious First Chief Directorate. Like the CIA, the SVR is responsible for collecting intelligence and covert operations outside its country's borders. Included in the SVR hierarchy was an international department that coordinated with foreign intelligence agencies on matters of mutual interest. SVR headquarters, known during Soviet times as the Center, was in Yasenevo, a forested area in the outskirts of Moscow.

Ministry of Internal Affairs (MVD): A largely uniformed service, the MVD is a national law enforcement agency that is charged with addressing a multitude of crimes, public disturbances, and combatting extremism. It is also responsible for enforcing immigration, drug laws, and traffic control. In the early 2000s, the MVD had a contingent of investigators dedicated to complex terrorism and organized crime cases, although those departments took a back seat to their counterparts in the FSB.

Prosecutor General's Office (PGO): Roughly equivalent to the US Department of Justice, the PGO's principal mission is to prosecute violations of Russian law. Unlike the Department of Justice, which is part of the executive branch in the US system, the Russian PGO is theoretically independent of the executive, legislative, and judicial branches of government.

Despite new challenges, I had a much more comfortable life in Moscow. My apartment was a two-minute walk to the embassy's main entrance, and there were no more road trips to third-world countries. Now my road trips were to FBIHQ, the FBI Academy, and the National

Counterterrorism Center to facilitate meetings and training exchanges with my new FSB colleagues. There were also FSB-sponsored trips to distant Russian cities and conferences with representatives of dozens of intelligence agencies from across the globe. Unlike in Kazakhstan, in Moscow, I had two highly motivated and able ALATs, both of whom had solid backgrounds and proved to be highly competent partners whose opinions I deeply respected.[10]

In my free time, I could revisit the Conservatory, the Russian ballet, and explore what had become a city rich in excellent restaurants. It was "hello" to the beautiful Moscow metro and "goodbye" to driving in the Almaty house-of-mirrors madhouse. At the time of my arrival, Moscow had just celebrated its 850th birthday, having been established when Europe was in the Dark Ages, before the Black Plague, and a couple hundred years before Columbus discovered the new world. In 2005 Moscow had all the comforts of home.

At the time of my arrival, Alexander Vershbow (whom I never met) was in the last days of his tour as US ambassador to Russia. He was replaced by Ambassador William J. Burns, a career State Department diplomat who was truly one of the most impressive people I had ever met—charismatic, a quiet but unassuming gentleman, soft-spoken and decisive, with a deep knowledge of all things Russian and an uncanny ability to connect with people on a personal level. Ambassador Burns and his deputy chief of mission were the embassy officials to whom I reported.[11]

US Embassy territory in Moscow is a self-contained, walled complex. Looming above everything is the heart of the complex—the modern embassy building that includes offices of State Department foreign service officers, attachés, and a host of other federal agencies. In 2005, positioned inside the exterior walls of the complex within a short walk to the embassy's main entrance were over 140 apartments—home to US citizens who worked in the embassy and their families. Within the complex were various security levels. The first floor of the embassy was at the lowest security level and included walkways to the cafeteria, grocery store, a travel agency, a full gym, a large pool, a video store, post office, ATMs, a bank, a laundry service, a bar, medical offices, a gift shop, and shoeshine stand. It was a city unto itself, where all the comforts of home were at our fingertips. And who staffed the bulk of these nonsecure facilities? Was it cleared Americans subject to rigorous background checks? No! In July 2005, when I arrived in Moscow, included among the US Embassy's many employees were approximately 743 foreign service nationals (FSNs)—locally employed staff (mostly Russians) who provided necessary services such as preparing meals, providing security at the points of entry, and staffing the gym, the travel agency, and the grocery and video stores. Also included among the FSN staff were highly educated professionals who worked in partnership with American diplomats in support of everyday tasks such as language instruction, document translation, and facilitating interactions between US federal agencies and their Russian counterparts. And let us not forget the cadre of locally employed tradesmen whose job was to maintain our living quarters—heating and cooling systems, electric, and plumbing—who had broad access to our apartments. There is not a shred of doubt in my mind that among the latter were those whose ancillary duties included repairing and adjusting the FSB-monitored audio and video devices secreted within our homes.

The 743 FSNs working inside the walls of the US Embassy compound in Moscow were a bit of a contrast to the number of American citizens working within the walls of the Russian Embassy in Washington, DC. The score? 743–0. To my knowledge, there were no Americans regularly assigned to work on Russian Embassy territory. So what's the deal? Did the Russians have an intelligence-gathering advantage over their American counterparts? Maybe, especially when one considers that FSNs had mothers, fathers, spouses, siblings, sons, and daughters who were vulnerable to the power and influence of the FSB. What type of coercion might a Russian citizen working in the American Embassy have faced? Imagine an FSN whose son or brother was nearing his eighteenth birthday, the mandatory military conscription age. In those days (as now) the Russian military had a credible reputation for brutally hazing the hundreds of thousands of conscripts forced into the military every year; hazing was so sadistic that it led to the formation of high-profile mothers' groups that publicized and protested the gross mistreatment of their conscripted sons. Most conscripts were poorly supplied and could expect to be sent far from home, where they led primitive lives and were sometimes responsible for growing their own food or sometimes sent off to war. How far would a parent, spouse, or sibling have gone to avoid such a fate for a loved one? Helping a child get into a choice university might have been another incentive, as might a relative's promotion at work.

All of these are examples of how the FSB's enormous power and control within Russian society could have been used to pressure an FSN into providing assistance, and thus be in a position to extend its tentacles deep into the embassy. But what kind of assistance might an FSN have been in a position to provide? Sometimes, seemingly trivial bits of information can be useful to an intelligence adversary: Who has a grievance against their boss? Who is having an extramarital affair? Whose spouse has a gambling problem? Who is having financial difficulties? What are embassy officials' personal weaknesses? The list and the possibilities are endless. Sometimes, simply eavesdropping on a casual conversation can be a goldmine. Is this to say that the FSN community was (or is) a nest of spies, purposefully planted by the FSB to betray their American employers and colleagues? Absolutely not! But a knock on the door from the FSB will send shivers up the spine of any Russian. In short, when one is in the business of gathering information, knowledge is power. And with 743 extremely vulnerable pairs of eyes and ears in place, the FSB had a target-rich environment for collecting intelligence.

The regional security officer (RSO), an on-site law enforcement officer / security advisor with the US Department of Diplomatic Security, enforced a host of rules governing life in the US Embassy, including access to the embassy compound.[12] Under his or her supervision, uniformed FSN guards inspected the identification of all persons entering the compound, and metal detectors and X-rays were in place at each of the two entrances. Invited guests seeking entrance into the embassy, including both US and non-US citizens, were required to turn over their passports, sign in and out, and be escorted by their US-citizen embassy host. All non-American citizens and those US citizens lacking specific security clearances were prohibited from accessing secure areas within the complex. And only US citizen guests, accompanied by their US-citizen, embassy-resident hosts, were allowed to stay overnight at embassy employees' apartments. But of all the embassy security functions, the Marine Security Guards had the most critical mission: twenty-four seven oversight of the many formidable layers of security that went into safeguarding classified equipment and the sacred scrolls (classified documents) that were maintained in highly protected areas. Those secure areas were accessible only to authorized US officials with the highest security clearance and a need to know.

Not only was the embassy guarded by US-controlled security, but strategically located immediately outside of each embassy entrance, on Russian soil, was a small guard station that housed a uniformed FSB officer twenty-four seven. At this officer's discretion, one had to show identification and/or submit to other forms of harassment upon entering or exiting the embassy grounds. There is no doubt that the FSB officers were keeping detailed logs of who came and went, with whom, at what times, and with particular attention given to known and/or suspected US intelligence officers and any Russian citizens who entered the complex. It is also safe to assume that the FSB guards closely coordinated with well-placed hidden FSB lookouts that were strategically located in buildings surrounding the embassy. But with respect to the FBI, the FSB guards' role as American antagonists clashed with another facet of the FSB's paradoxical relationship with the FBI—a relationship that cut both ways.

Prior to my return to Moscow in 2005, those who preceded me in the legat office had set the bar pretty high. My immediate predecessor was a brilliant agent with a solid background in Italian and Russian Mafia investigations. With his New York flair, he sometimes referred to Russia itself as the quintessential criminal organization. He spoke excellent Russian, knew Russian culture well, and jokingly complained to me of being exhausted by the many "bear hugs" he'd endured as legat. His ALAT was a well-respected, hard-working former partner of mine from our days as street agents in San Francisco. For all those reasons, it was no surprise to me that during their tenure, my predecessors set the gold standard by putting together the type of case to which I aspired:

Hemant Lakhani was a London-based rice trader and a sometimes-legal arms trader born in India. In 2003 he came to the attention of the FBI through an FBI informant who shared a mutual acquaintance with Lakhani. From conversations with the FBI informant, Lakhani came to believe that the informant was affiliated with a Somali terrorist group in search of shoulder-fired weapons to attack US civilian airliners. Lakhani claimed to be able to supply such weapons and agreed to locate a sample for the FBI informant. In that effort, Lakhani initially reached out to a legitimate, state-owned Ukrainian arms company with which he had previously done business. Having failed in that initial attempt, Lakhani turned to a Cyprus arms company with a questionable reputation, with offices in Kyiv and Moscow. As he was attempting to locate a source for said missiles, Lakhani caught the attention of FSB officers, who introduced a Russian undercover officer posing as a disgruntled soldier in a position to supply the weapons Lakhani was seeking.[13]

My predecessors' involvement with the Lakhani investigation began in the usual fashion, with a request from FBI Newark for information from the Russians. In the course of preparing its response, the legat office learned of the FSB's shared interest in Lakhani and arranged for the FSB to coordinate its investigation with that of the FBI in Newark. At the conclusion of this joint operation, Lakhani traveled from Russia to the US, where he presented the FBI informant with an (inert) surface-to-air missile that had been supplied to him by Lakhani's Russian "contact." Lakhani was then arrested, tried in US court, and sentenced to forty-seven years in prison. One critical government witness was an FSB colonel who provided testimony in US court on Lakhani's actions in Russia.

The Hemant Lakhani investigation was a textbook case on how things are supposed to work in legat land. It was a great example of how, in a perfect world, the FBI and the FSB were able to mutually benefit from working together. As such, it was also a perfect example of the golden middle, where the interests of the FSB and FBI overlapped. But this happy-ending, perfect-world scenario was the antithesis of the other side of the FBI-FSB "relationship" in which those of us in the legat office were a captive audience on FSB turf.

CHAPTER 8

The Quieter You Go, the Farther You Get

Тише едешь, дальше будешь

As US-BASED FBI STREET AGENTS, WE WERE THE HUNTERS, AND AS WE pursued our investigations, we were careful not to let our targets see us coming until we had our virtual teeth in their virtual jugular. But in Moscow, despite the productive side of the FBI-FSB relationship, those of us in sensitive embassy positions were the hunted, with our pursuers being FSB officers who used many of the same sophisticated tools and time-tested strategies we as FBI agents used at home. In short, as we were working hand in hand with our FSB partners on areas of mutual interest, we had to assume that their counterintelligence counterparts were targeting us both as a means of recruiting us as future FSB spies and/or catching us in the act of conducting clandestine intelligence operations.

It was with this mindset that I made some logical assumptions about our FSB adversaries: like successful FBI agents, FSB officers believed wholeheartedly in their mission. From their perspective, successfully recruiting a member of the US intelligence community or catching a member of the US intelligence community in an act of spying would be a crowning achievement in support of a noble cause. I had no doubt that they were hungry, smart, well trained, and proud of the organization they represented. That pride stemmed, in part, from the fact that they had state-of-the-art tools at their disposal, allowing them to gather intelligence without being detected. That kept us off balance, never sure of when or where we were in their sights. It also forced us to be ever mindful of our surroundings, which, over time, is exhausting. And so as the hunted, we found it essential to bear in mind the ways in which the FSB could use those sophisticated tools and time-tested strategies against us.

For the FSB, recruiting insiders within an adversary's organization—human intelligence—is the most direct and effective means of penetrating the heart of their rival's operations. The most valuable informants are insiders in a position to provide classified information and documents relating to an organization's strategies, methods, sources, means of communication, and vulnerabilities. But recruiting informants does not take place in a vacuum and is typically built on gathering extensive information about a potential source's personal weaknesses, vulnerabilities, and motivations. And so like any American in Moscow—government official or businessman—it would have been foolish for us to underestimate the importance that Russians place on gathering *kompromat*—compromising information that can be used as blackmail. In the words of Charles Colson, "If you got 'em by the balls, their hearts and minds will always follow."[1]

As in investigations of any criminal organization, in the spy business, knowledge is power, and the FSB's ability to gather that knowledge included their ability to intercept all but our most encrypted, highly classified communications. The most vulnerable communications included our face-to-face conversations, personal cellphone and hardline telephone communications, and unclassified texts and emails, supplemented by intrusions into any electronic devices left unattended in our apartments—laptops, cellphones, or desktop computers. In addition to interceptions of our personal conversations, the FSB's wide net likely included intercepting our associates' communications to determine what was being said about us—a backdoor means of gathering intelligence. As a result, every one of our associates, including spouses, was a potential source of information, whether witting (knowingly providing information) or unwitting (unknowingly revealing information, oblivious to the possibility that the FSB might be listening).

Video feeds were another aspect of technical surveillance that likely tracked what we did in our apartments and on the embassy grounds, outside of which stood several tall buildings. One nearby structure, an old church with a bell tower that doubled as our morning wake-up call, was known to us as the "Church of the Immaculate Reception" for its ideal location as a listening post to intercept our conversations and track our movements. In short, not only did life in the embassy fishbowl limit our ability to maintain our privacy from one another, but it was often difficult to privately communicate with anyone without FSB intrusion. As they dissected our conversations, FSB officers were undoubtedly in search of a path to the *kompromat* that fueled their spy-recruiting mission.

Physical surveillance was also a given, augmenting the FSB's ability to determine our habits, associates, and hangouts. Tracking the movements of American Embassy employees was everywhere and in various forms, both within and outside of the embassy walls. In some cases surveillance outside the embassy was conducted in plain sight, in which case the FSB wanted to be seen, either as a message or a warning. That was especially true in the case of officials who fell into a special category known in Russian as the *siloviki*—high-ranking members of powerful security services, military, and/or law enforcement. Those of us who fell into that category were prime FSB targets. In other cases surveillance was clandestine. What was the objective? To catch us doing something we were trying to hide for reasons either personal or professional. In this effort, the FSB had the perfect starting point—the guard posts immediately outside the embassy exits from which they could begin tracking our movements the moment we left the embassy grounds.

One thing our FSB keepers were likely looking for were signs of clandestine operations: efforts to recruit, communicate with, or meet Russian sources. Their focus also likely included identifying *dead drops*—clandestine, prearranged sites used to exchange documents and/or collect information from or make payments to sources. I cannot speak for anyone else, but FSB efforts to uncover clandestine operations on my part were a waste of time. Most of what my office did was transparent, and we were guided by a motto my predecessor passed on to me: "No lyin,' no spyin.'" We did not recruit spies or meet with Russian sources, nor did we have clandestine meetings.

Combined with technical surveillance, physical surveillance helps answer questions such as where and when we might be alone—critical information if the FSB was planning an "accidental" meeting and/or building up to a pitch (a direct solicitation for assistance). Together, those techniques also had the potential to answer questions such as what skeletons were in our closet, what were our financial needs, and what were our private pleasures or personal weaknesses (i.e., what aspects of our personal lives would we not want to see on the front page of the *New York Times!*). Another valuable tidbit might have been our career aspirations—what direction we hoped our careers might take in the future—a potential goldmine for planning a recruitment years down the road, when we might be in a more powerful or influential position. In short, it is safe to assume that the FSB used every tool to learn every bit of information imaginable, including seemingly trivial details—a powerful psychological tool as the hunter attempts to intimidate his target by convincing him or her that he or she is the center of the hunter's universe.

With a wealth of intelligence at their fingertips, FSB officers would then be in a position to formulate a strategy—a ready-in-waiting recruitment approach that was limited only by an FSB officer's creative imagination. In the case of the FBI, legal and internal policy restrictions are clear and binding when planning any investigative strategy, and penalties for violating those boundaries are harsh. But in the case of the FSB, not so much. What kind of pitch might an FSB officer have used to lure his target into providing information? Should they have used a carrot or a stick? Typically, this was the time when knowledge of our personal needs, weaknesses, and vulnerabilities came into play. If coercion was not the primary strategy, was there an indication that the target might be motivated to volunteer information? Was he or she in need of financial help? Might he have been motivated to satisfy a grudge against his organization? Or might a simpler approach have worked—playing on his susceptibility to flattery or appeal to a fragile ego?

Armed with information about our weaknesses, vulnerabilities, and motivations, it is logical to assume that FSB officers were prepared to use that information to lure (or pressure) us into cooperating. In this effort there is little doubt that they were trained to build relationships with their targets through engaging interpersonal skills and a solid understanding of human nature. They likely understood that the most superficial contact with their target is the beginning of a rapport and that nurturing that rapport is built on being a good listener and a careful observer, able to pick up on nonverbal clues. In so doing, it is safe to assume that they were taught to connect one-on-one, make eye contact, and portray an image of someone their target could eventually learn to trust, even if that "trust" came with an unpleasant aftertaste.

In many ways these are the same skills that a professional psychologist, psychiatrist, or social worker masters to help a client overcome emotional suffering and/or navigate a personal struggle. But for an FSB intelligence officer, the dark side of these skills is their potential use as a tool to gain cooperation by simultaneously creating pain and building trust—to convince their target that their cooperation, though not a pleasant choice, might eventually lead to some reward and remain confidential. When all was said and done, there was always good reason to believe that the eyes and ears of the FSB were lurking somewhere, in search of blood in the water.

As a San Francisco-based case agent whose focus was organized crime, I had a good sense of how the FSB was targeting those of us in the US intelligence community. Over my career I had bugged just about every device and location imaginable: businesses, cellphones, pay phones, and potted plants on public sidewalks, where our subjects huddled every night at 2:00 a.m., away from the public eye, to plan whatever it was they were planning. But unlike our FSB counterparts, each time that I (or any FBI agent) intruded into the privacy of a criminal target, we were subject to a litany of rigorous legal procedures. In the case of the most invasive tool, electronic surveillance, gaining legal approval for wiretaps was a painstaking process that typically took place after demonstrating to a federal judge that all other avenues of investigation had failed to accomplish investigative goals—a system designed as a barrier against unwarranted intrusions into the privacy of any US person. The early stages of the application process included a detailed request for electronic surveillance that incorporated legal requirements such as targets' identities, distinct crimes, and the specific means of communication used to commit those crimes. Next came a careful review of a draft affidavit attesting to facts supporting probable cause and necessity by a string of government attorneys. From there the agent's soon-to-be-sworn affidavit faced intense judicial scrutiny, followed by a federal judge's required written authorization. Once electronic surveillance began, the entire process was subject to meticulous postapproval oversight by that same judge. And at the conclusion of each investigation, we were placed under a microscope by a bevy of well-funded defense attorneys, hungry to identify legal misrepresentations in our sworn affidavits and/or improper conduct on our part, with the potential for career-ending consequences and/or devastating legal repercussions.

As one intimately familiar with wiretaps, I knew that in Moscow, every time I spoke, I had to carefully consider whether what I was saying might be of interest to the FSB. Unfortunately, the people with whom we spoke on the telephone did not always share that mindset. That was sometimes true of FBI field agents, who were careless over the phone. Those were the guys who would call from the US over unsecure lines to discuss criminal investigations with a Russian nexus. I couldn't help but be amused when they would conclude our discussion by asking me not to tell the Russians the details of our conversation. My response? "I don't have to; you just did."

You've got to hand it to the FSB for their creativity; they always found inventive ways to communicate to the American *siloviki* that they had free rein in our lives and homes. One of the foulest yet most effective means of communication was their way of saying, "Just dropped in to say hello!"—the practice of leaving welcome-home surprises in the toilet bowl. An equally offensive Russian calling card was an ice cube tray filled with urine, which was FSB shorthand for any number of messages directed at the unfortunate recipient. A less juvenile but no less galling FSB ploy came in the form of a string of poles installed immediately outside the exterior perimeter of the embassy compound on Russian territory. What was the Russians' explanation? The poles were being installed for our safety, to be used as platforms for outward-facing security cameras. In a classic case of "Don't p—s on my foot and tell me it's raining," the obvious purpose was the posts' potential usefulness as inward-directed surveillance platforms, given that they ringed the entire compound and could easily be set up to intercept our conversations, track our movements, or as a more sinister attempt at gathering intelligence from within the embassy.

As street agents, we were often guided by the expression "It's only paranoia if you're wrong." At times we were convinced our surveillance targets had "made us"—that is, detected our surveillance. Sometimes this was just plain paranoia. But if we were right, that meant making an adjustment. It was time to double up on being smart, cautious, and careful or to invent a ruse to give the subjects something to hang their hat on, to relieve them of their paranoia and put them at ease. But if truth be told, when one lives in an environment without privacy and under constant surveillance, mistrust and paranoia are occupational hazards.

CHAPTER 9

The Only Free Cheese Is in the Mousetrap

Бесплатный сыр бывает только в мышеловке

HONEYTRAPS HAVE LONG BEEN AMONG THE RUSSIANS' MOST BASIC YET effective means of blackmailing Americans into cooperation. Having been on the receiving end of one such attempt following an organized crime conference, I find it's not hard to see why. The encounter took place at an outdoor cafe in Moscow's Old Arbat district after a week of daylong meetings with Russian law enforcement officials. After lunch an attractive young interpreter quietly asked me if I would like to bring her back to my room. I swallowed hard but declined her generous offer. When she "innocently" asked me why, I just smiled and replied, "Kompromat!" Had I somehow turned into a handsome movie star? No! Did I walk away because I was married? (I wasn't.) Was it because I didn't find her seriously attractive? (I did.) Maybe it was because of my soaring moral standards. (Let's not go there!) One good reason for walking away was instinctive, plain and simple. I knew that there would be pictures of this young woman and me available for use against me then or years down the road, depending on when it would be most advantageous for the FSB. That assumption was bolstered by a cautionary tale I read about a few years later.

As part of an embassy security briefing, I was informed of a similar incident involving a visiting government official who'd traveled to Russia for a seminar with a Russian government agency. During the seminar the visitor became quite comfortable with his new Russian colleagues and, during an event celebrating the successful conclusion of the seminar, shared with them a few toasts. As it happened, there was a Russian woman at the celebration whom the visitor found quite attractive. Did I mention that he was married? Where it went from there is obvious. The next morning, as he was preparing to return home, one of his new Russian "friends" met him privately and casually brought up the subject of the visitor's wife. Then going in for the kill, the Russian official pulled out compromising photos of the visitor and his newfound girlfriend. As he did so, he asked, "How do you think your wife would feel about these?" No doubt the visitor's lower region slammed shut loud enough to be heard for miles. The next day he did the right thing, as difficult as that might have been, by filing a detailed report of the incident with his embassy's security officer. Need I say more?

But the FSB had options. They could have quietly held on to the photos for a more opportune moment when, down the road, the official might have held a more sensitive position. The FSB is notorious for this simple but extremely effective strategy. In either case, the goal would be to turn the victim, to get him (or her) to work clandestinely for the FSB and against the interests of his or her country. In the case of any American official, this would be, of course, a serious crime under US law. But this tactic is not just reserved for diplomats and visiting government officials. It is equally useful and effective against businessmen who travel to Russia, especially those who are of current or future value to the Russians through their ability to affect government policy and/or gain access to classified information. And so this cautionary tale is directed at anyone traveling to Russia who has or aspires to have a position of power and/or influence either within a government agency or in the private sector.

Having spent considerable time in Moscow, Central Asia, Hungary, and other former Soviet Bloc countries, I was used to the unanticipated hazards associated with honeytraps, mousetraps, and landmines. But Moscow was a popular destination for FBI agents traveling to Russia for the first time to share in "best practices" exchanges with the FSB or MVD or for face-to-face meetings with Russian counterparts related to specific cases. As a result, it was my responsibility to give "how to survive

Moscow" safety briefings to my colleagues upon their arrival. As a rule, those briefings went something like this:

1. The most dangerous thing you can do is cross the street.

2. Everything you say and do is being monitored.

3. If you see a wad of cash fall out of someone's pocket, keep walking.

4. Don't go anywhere alone, and be sure that everyone knows where you are.

5. Don't be tricked into thinking you suddenly developed movie-star good looks.

6. Stay away from Night Flight.

Of my admonitions I was confident I would not have issues with numbers one to four. Number five was questionable, but Night Flight, Moscow's most notorious nightclub, was another matter. This venue had a reputation as a place not to be believed until seen. If Americans had not already heard of it, it was *the* place their hotel concierge suggested they visit. I used to lose sleep over having to get agents on temporary duty (lacking diplomatic status) out of jail or out of the hospital, followed by endless explanations to the FBI Security Division and the embassy's regional security officer. I'm happy to say that there were never any issues with any of the above concerns.

As mousetraps go, honeytraps had the potential for obvious, serious consequences. It was not only a technique used against intelligence adversaries and American businessmen but also internal political enemies—Russian officials in high places who had fallen out of favor and later found videos of their indiscretions in mass media stories. But for those of us in the legat office, not all "free cheese" was taboo, and as we sampled some of the FSB's "free cheese," we came to appreciate that "in every joke, there is a measure of truth" (В каждой шутке есть доля правды):

A florist walks into a barbershop for a haircut. When it comes time to pay, the barber says, "No, no! For you, the haircut is free!" The florist is pleasantly surprised but confused. He asks why. The barber replies, "Because you bring so much beauty into the world with your wonderful bouquets—the delightful smells, the rich colors. Your haircut is my way of saying thank you for your many gifts." The florist walks out of the shop with a great haircut and a huge smile. And what does the barber find the next morning when he arrives at work? Dozens of bouquets of beautiful, fresh flowers!

The next day a baker comes to the same barber for a haircut. After his haircut he reaches into his pocket to pay. As in the case of the florist, the barber says, "No, no, no! For you, the haircut is free." And like the florist, the baker, amazed at the barber's generosity, asks why. The barber explains that the baker brings so much joy to the world with his delicious, clever creations and that he just wishes to show his appreciation. The baker thanks the barber profusely. The next morning the barber arrives at work to discover platters full of delicious pastries.

On the third day, an FBI agent comes to the same barber for a haircut. Like the florist and the baker before him, he pulls out his cash to pay and the barber says, "No, no. Absolutely not! For you, the haircut is free." And like the florist and the barber before him, the befuddled FBI agent asks why. And once again, the barber explains that the agent makes the world a safer place; he protects the innocent and makes sacrifices for his country. Like the florist and the barber before him, the FBI agent leaves the shop with a huge smile on his face. And what does the barber find when he arrives at work the next morning? Five more FBI agents.

That pretty much sums up my reaction to the many lavish official banquets we attended that were hosted by the FSB, always in historic settings with sumptuous hors d'oeuvres and even a few laughs. As hosts, they were professionals; they knew how to keep the evening moving, ensuring that everyone was dazzled by the meals and entertainment. And yet I couldn't help but wonder whether they were trying to send another message: This was no longer the 1990s of Boris Yeltsin, and this was no longer a starving, struggling young Russian Federation. Russia and the KGB were back, well funded and powerful.

CHAPTER 10

The Fall and Rise of Chekism

AUGUST IN RUSSIA IS TYPICALLY A VERY SLOW MONTH, AND FOR AMER-
icans working in the US Embassy, it is a challenge to get anything done.
It's a time when most Muscovites travel outside the city, many spending weeks in their country homes, which is made evident by the steady
stream of cars heading out of the city. The weather is usually hot and
sticky, and generally speaking, there is not a lot going on. And with little
happening, few Russians are paying attention—unless, for some reason,
they are jolted back to reality.

On August 19, 1991, Soviet citizens awoke to strangely foreboding
television programming: *Swan Lake* was playing over and over, just as
it had after the deaths of Soviet leaders Leonid Brezhnev, Konstantin
Chernenko, and Yuri Andropov. This was a subtle signal that new leadership was about to assume control of the Soviet Union; ironically yet
darkly reminiscent of the symbolism behind the release of white smoke
over the Sistine Chapel to announce the election of a new pope. What
Soviets were soon to discover was that their leader, Mikhail Gorbachev,
had been arrested while on vacation at his dacha on the Black Sea. In fact,
a coup was underway, led by a group of hardline Soviet officials including
KGB chairman Vladimir Kryuchkov, who believed Gorbachev's reform
policies had gone too far. The coup ultimately failed, eventually contributing to the disbanding of the KGB and, soon after, the breakup of
the Soviet Union. Three days after the failed coup, a large statue of the
KGB's most revered strongman, Iron Felix, which had stood outside the
KGB's Lubyanka headquarters since 1958, was torn down. According to

Milt Bearden, coauthor of *The Main Enemy*, after its removal, someone wrote a message on the statue's pedestal: "Dear Felix. We are sorry that we couldn't save you. But you will remain with us."[1]

That statue was subsequently taken to a statue graveyard that I visited in 1998. There, along with Iron Felix, I witnessed the sleeping statues of other former Soviet icons, including that of Josef Stalin (see figure 10.1), who was, by then, an object of derision by those who cheered the dissolution of the Soviet Union. But that did not include all former Soviets, especially those who had survived the Great Patriotic War, many of whom saw the disbanding of the KGB and the dissolution of the Soviet Union as tragedies. Nor did it include the many former Soviets who were still mourning the loss of their cherished superpower status. Within days of the coup, Chairman Kryuchkov of the KGB was arrested and subsequently sent to prison. In theory, with his arrest, Russia had seen the last

Figure 10.1. Fallen Statue of Josef Stalin, Moscow, 1998.
SOURCE: AUTHOR'S PERSONAL COLLECTION

of the KGB. But the world should have known better. And that certainly included me.

After months of steady contact with the FSB, it became increasingly clear to me that FSB officers were rediscovering a growing sense of pride under Putin, which was in sharp contrast to the humiliation those true believers had suffered in 1991. For FSB officers, the events of 1991 were personal. Not only had they failed in their sacred duty to protect the Soviet Union, but their nemesis, Mikhail Gorbachev, had added insult to injury by dismembering their beloved KGB. But by the time I returned to Moscow in 2005, their growing confidence and camaraderie were on full display each December 20 as I witnessed FSB officers proudly congratulating each other (and me, with a note of sarcasm) with the greeting "C Dnyom Chekista" (Day of the Chekist), a day of celebration originally established during the early days of the Bolshevik Revolution. That tribute to each other and the ghosts of Chekists past sprang from the FSB's Soviet heritage: the power and duty, using any means necessary, to protect the power structure and the unique social experiment that grew out of the revolution. As such, that simple greeting was also a way of connecting with their kindred spirits, not just past and present but future.

In hindsight, I should have realized that this newfound FSB confidence reflected a broader sense of pride that would have deep implications for Russia and, by extension, for the United States. What I did not fully appreciate at the time was the power of the Soviet Union's lingering shadow to influence Russia's future. Had I understood more about Soviet history, I may have better understood how the Soviet Union's iron grip on its citizens would become a springboard to Russia's future and how Russia's gradual return to its Soviet roots would one day reseed tensions between Russia and the West. Years later, as I continued to follow Moscow's political trajectory, it became ever more disconcerting to watch aspects of our internal American dialogue take on familiar echoes of Soviet political slogans and strategies for holding on to power. And so began my attempt to answer the question of why we, as Americans, should care about the history of a country that no longer exists. In my attempt to answer that question, it became clear how essential it is to appreciate what it looks like when an aspiring democracy gradually unravels as one person's lust for power and his followers' thirst for a strongman leader combine to degrade the checks and balances, freedom of the press, respect for human rights, free and fair elections, and rule of law that hold a democracy together.

Chekism is the common thread that binds the early Soviet Union to today's Russia. Chekist power sprang from the 1917 Bolshevik Revolution with the creation of the All Russian Extraordinary Commission—the Soviet Union's first secret police organization. In the 1930s the Chekist thread took the form of the NKVD (the People's Commissariat for Internal Affairs), which, after several iterations, was rebranded into the KGB in 1954. With the disbanding of the KGB in 1991, Chekism was transformed into today's FSB (and SVR). Labels aside, Chekists were always charged with controlling Soviet and, later, Russian society. Some historians consider Chekists to have been the true power behind the Soviet Union, rivaling that of the Communist Party. In modern times some Soviet experts see Putin's twenty-first-century step into the presidency as the "culmination of the KGB's crusade for power."[2] And in case anyone missed Putin's commitment to that crusade and his position as its flag bearer, upon assuming the role of prime minister in 1999, during a speech to his former FSB comrades on the Day of the Chekist, Vladimir Putin wryly joked that their first undercover mission to infiltrate the (Russian) government was in the process of completing its task.[3]

Chekism has a sordid history, beginning with its role in protecting the Bolshevik Revolution. The mission of early Chekists was to preserve the revolutionary order by preventing sabotage of the revolution and combating counterrevolutionaries. Their mission also included fighting crimes such as banditry and speculation (engaging in private enterprise). During the Red Terror of 1918 and, later, Soviet leader Josef Stalin's Great Purge of the 1930s, hundreds of thousands of Soviets accused of opposing the Bolsheviks were subject to secret arrests, torture, and execution without trial. A military arm of Chekism ran the gulags—Soviet prisons—where military deserters, accused dissidents, and counterrevolutionaries were housed, tortured, and executed. The Chekist leader largely responsible for building that brutal system was Felix Dzerzhinsky, nicknamed "Iron Felix" for his cold-blooded enforcement and unflinching devotion to the revolution.

During a speech in 1917, Iron Felix introduced the term "enemies of the people"—a politically expedient, loaded phrase that Stalin exploited throughout his thirty-one years as leader of the Soviet Union. By artfully implying that he spoke for the people when using this expression, Stalin cleverly inferred that he was speaking on behalf of the majority of Soviet citizens. In fact, the phrase was a carefully crafted means of vilifying, terrifying, and destroying those he perceived as his personal and political enemies. Among the "enemies of the people" were the capitalist class that once controlled Russia's wealth and means of production, the Russian Orthodox Church, and anyone who opposed and/or threatened the power of the Communist Party. As part of a brutal crackdown on his enemies, Stalin also used the phrase to target once loyal allies if they dared to get in his way. After Stalin's death in 1953, during a secret speech to the Twentieth Communist Party Congress in 1956, Soviet leader Nikita Khrushchev condemned the "cult of personality" built around Stalin and his use of the term "enemies of the people," which he described as contributing to the "cruel repression" of Soviet citizens.[4]

In the early days of the Cold War, Chekism morphed into the KGB, this time with a new, heavy-handed role in emerging Soviet Bloc countries that followed the punishing suppression of a million-strong uprising in East Germany in 1953. In coordination with its kindred spirits in Eastern Bloc countries, the KGB monitored public and private opinion behind the Iron Curtain with an eye toward uncovering plots to overthrow Soviet-friendly governments. With Soviet tanks as enforcers, the KGB and its Eastern Bloc surrogates crushed the uprising in Hungary in 1956 and put down the 1968 Prague Spring revolt in Czechoslovakia. The KGB later took part in the less-than-successful attempt to suppress the 1980s Solidarity labor movement in Poland.

The KGB emblem was a throwback to the Bolshevik Revolution, consisting of a sword and shield: the sword to destroy the enemies of the revolution, the shield to defend the revolution. Their motto was "Loyalty to the party. Loyalty to the Motherland."[5] The KGB was composed of external branches that were responsible for foreign operations and intelligence gathering; internal security branches with telltale titles such as the Political Security Service, Covert Surveillance, and Wiretapping; and a branch composed of paramilitary troops, including the KGB Alpha Team, which was responsible for using military tactics to address domestic threats. Within Soviet borders the KGB's wide-ranging domestic mission included tracking political dissidents, combating religious activities, and punishing anti-Soviet activities thought to be inspired by foreign powers. The KGB was also a major player in Soviet palace intrigue, having supported Leonid Brezhnev in the overthrow of Nikita Khrushchev in 1964.[6] During the 1970s and 1980s, the KGB crushed dissent using laws that criminalized "spreading rumors detrimental to the Soviet societal . . . structure"[7] and "spreading anti-Soviet propaganda."[8] Those ambiguously worded, all-encompassing statutes were ideal for criminalizing the actions of dissidents, such as novelist and Nobel laureate Alexander Solzhenitsyn and physicist and Nobel laureate Andrei Sakharov.

Lubyanka was the spiritual home of the Chekists. Built in 1898 near Catherine the Great's secret police headquarters, Lubyanka was the original Moscow Cheka headquarters, which, for good measure, included a prison where "enemies of the people" were subject to harsh interrogations, torture, and execution. In the mid-2000s, Lubyanka was still being used by the FSB as one of its headquarters offices and was also the home of the KGB Museum, which I visited with FSB guides in 2006.[9] That tour coincided with my most memorable visit to Lubyanka—an official conference held in the inner sanctum of that monument to Chekism: the meticulously preserved third-floor office of Yuri Andropov, head of the KGB from 1967 to 1982. (See figure 10.2.)

Yuri Vladimirovich Andropov was the quintessential guardian of the Bolshevik Revolution. He was a general in the Soviet Armed Forces, having begun his military service in 1939. From 1954 to 1957, he served as Soviet ambassador to Hungary, where he kept an eye on Soviet Armed Forces' cold-blooded crackdown on the 1956 uprising in Budapest. He was a member of the policymaking arm of the Communist Party (the Politburo) and chairman of the KGB from 1967 until 1982. In 1982 he replaced Leonid Brezhnev as leader of the Soviet Union.

Figure 10.2. Author at FSB HQ, Lubyanka, Moscow, 1998.
SOURCE: AUTHOR'S PERSONAL COLLECTION

As head of the KGB, Andropov led a vigorous crusade against internal political dissent, focused on "social undesirables" who were subject to forced commitment to psychiatric institutions, a strategy described as punitive psychiatry.[10] As the leader of the Soviet Union, he was known for resurrecting a Stalin-era policy in which a small army of citizen informers were secretly recruited to anonymously report on fellow citizens for drunkenness, antisocialist lifestyles, and/or failing to report to work. In some areas this policy of societal "self-purification" was enabled by Soviet police, who handed out thousands of prefilled cards to the citizenry, detailing a list of offenses fellow citizens might have committed—cards that could then be checkmarked and anonymously returned to the police.[11] It was also a common belief that each Soviet apartment building had at least one citizen informer with similar responsibilities. Such informers were humorously parodied in the Russian film *Diamond Arm* (Бриллиантовая рука), from which came the memorable line "Our people don't take taxis to the bakery" (Наши люди в булочную на такси не ездят), based on a scene in which a busybody's watchful eye catches her neighbor in an act of decadence by taking a taxi (rather than public transportation) to buy a loaf of bread.

The conference in Andropov's Lubyanka office was the culmination of a series of high-level exchanges between the FBI and FSB on several topics, which were mostly related to terrorism. But the symbolic importance of the conference paled in comparison to the symbolism represented by Andropov's office itself not just because of its historic significance but because of its decor: its imposing conference table, snow-white busts of Iron Felix, and Andropov's desk on which sat telephones and sharpened pencils just as he'd left them in 1982. This was Chekism's sacred temple, its spiritual home—a shrine to the KGB and Soviet ideology that had been meticulously preserved since 1982. Like the story line from a bad science fiction movie, Andropov's office appeared to have been waiting for a spark to bring it back to life. And beginning in March 2000, it did come back to life, with the spark being Putin's election to the office of president of the Russian Federation. And in case anyone missed the significance of his election, included among Putin's inaugural guests was Andropov protégé Vladimir Kryuchkov, former chairman of the KGB who led the 1991 coup against Gorbachev and had been released from prison in 1994.

But just how Putin engineered his ascendence to the office of president of the Russian Federation in the years preceding his election is a story unto itself.

If you've ever watched an expert con man run a shell game, you know how hard it is to pick which of the three shells hides the pea. Those on the sidelines sometimes get a sneak peek of the bright orange pea—no accident—to entice them into believing they've got the game figured out and to lay their money down. The occasional winner, often a shill who is in cahoots with the con man, convinces everyone that beating the con man isn't really so hard. But the con man is an expert; he knows how to distract, confuse, and manipulate. Everything is in motion, and his hands are quicker than your eye as he moves the pea at lightning speed, sometimes tricking players into believing the pea is somewhere it's not. In Putin's case, cleverly moving around the pea was a way of maintaining his hold on power.

Putin grew up in Leningrad (now St. Petersburg), where his parents suffered under the brutal Nazi siege during the Great Patriotic War. In 1975 he began his career with the KGB; his first assignment was that of a counterintelligence officer, after which he was responsible for monitoring foreigners affiliated with consulates in Leningrad. In 1985 he was transferred to Dresden, East Germany, where he had a near-front-row seat for the collapse of the Berlin Wall and allegedly fought off dissidents and looters who attacked the local KGB office as the wall fell. After the dissolution of the Soviet Union in 1991, Putin left the KGB with the rank of lieutenant colonel. Then a private citizen, he held various local government positions in St. Petersburg.

In August 1998 President Boris Yeltsin appointed Putin to the first of three powerful official positions he would eventually hold at Yeltsin's behest: chairman of the FSB. Putin's rapid ascent to power soon caught the attention of a wealthy oligarch (Boris Berezovsky), who, during a period of instability within the Russian government, encouraged Yeltsin to promote Putin from head of the FSB to acting prime minister. Yeltsin agreed and, after appointing Putin to that position, made the fateful decision on the last day of the millennium to immediately resign as president. That decision left Putin, Yeltsin's new acting prime minister, to step in as his replacement. (Immediately following Yeltsin's New Year's Eve announcement to the nation, Putin addressed millions of citizens on Russian TV, guaranteeing that their rights under the Russian constitution would remain intact.) Yeltsin's decision was founded, in part, on the belief that holding the position of acting president would put Putin in a position of strength against rival presidential candidates in the upcoming March 2000 election. The plan worked. Putin was elected to his first four-year term as president and was inaugurated in May 2000. What was his first presidential decree? Payback! A grant of immunity from criminal prosecution was given for Yeltsin and his family.[12] Putin was reelected to a second four-year term in 2004. In November 2005 he appointed Dmitry Medvedev to the position of first deputy prime minister.

In 2006, amid his second term as president, Putin faced a dilemma: how to get around a constitutional prohibition against running for a third consecutive term in 2008. Unable to run for president, Putin devised a shell game of his own, and like other master con men, he recruited an accomplice. Thus was born a transparent bait-and-switch arrangement with Dmitry Medvedev: Medvedev would run for president in 2008 as a placeholder for Putin and nominate Putin as his prime minister (which he did). The prime minister role is normally a position of lesser power, yet there was never a question as to which of the two leaders would remain the alpha male. And despite his supposed underdog position, Putin continued to hold tightly onto the reins of power. Having won the 2008 presidential election, Medvedev, as predicted, declined to run for a second term in 2012. The door was then wide open for Putin to reclaim his position as president. But Medvedev had sweetened the pot: six months after his 2008 election as president, Medvedev sponsored a bill extending the presidential term from four to six years. What was the end result? Medvedev's future replacement (Putin) could serve another two six-year terms (twelve years total) as president if he were elected in 2012.

Putin won the 2012 presidential election despite significant chaos and noisy prodemocracy demonstrations. And as planned, Putin and Medvedev once again switched roles. With Putin's return to the presidency, the shell game continued as he nominated Medvedev to the office of prime minister for the 2012–2018 term. Now, thanks to Medvedev, Putin was able to hold office for two additional six-year terms, allowing for the possibility that he would remain president until 2024. Under Putin (who won his bid for reelection in 2018), Medvedev held the position of prime minister until 2020, when he resigned from that position, allegedly to give Putin a free hand to make broad changes to the Russian constitution.[13] In 2020, to the surprise of no one, Russian voters approved an amendment to the Russian constitution allowing Putin to hold office for two additional six-year terms, extending the limit of his potential term from 2024 to 2036. That blatant manipulation of the Russian constitution prompted Patriarch Kirill, the head of the Russian Orthodox Church, to describe Putin's tenure as a "miracle of God."[14] In all, if he should choose to do so, Putin will have remained in top leadership positions for a total of thirty-six years. So much for the original intent of the 1993 Russian constitution, which, with help from Russia's legislature, bent to the will of its autocratic leader. And with no real term limits and no visible threat of being forced out of office, Putin is free to continue executing his plan: reassembling the once-broken pieces of the former Soviet Union and rebuilding the Russian Empire. What was Putin's next move? Take control of the narrative.

CHAPTER 11

Back to the USSR

THE SOCIETY OF PROFESSIONAL JOURNALISTS IS THE OLDEST PROFES-
sional journalism organization in the US. Its preamble in part states,
"Public enlightenment is the forerunner of justice and the foundation
of democracy."[1] Its code of ethics can be summarized with four basic
journalistic principles: Seek the truth and report it. Minimize harm. Act
independently. Be accountable and transparent. These are lofty ideals and,
in a democracy, help to hold the government's feet to the fire. Under this
approach to journalism, those reporting the news answer only to their
professional standards, their conscience, and the public. In so doing,
they help to promote a civil, fact-based open discourse while holding
the government accountable to carry out its functions according to the
Constitution and written laws. These are difficult standards to achieve
and maintain, especially given today's polarized programming in which,
like with candy vending machines, we pick and choose which "facts" and
opinions we prefer to consume. And all too often, those "facts" appeal to
our emotions over intellect, fail to challenge our thinking, and instead
encourage us to take the path of least resistance by reinforcing our personal beliefs and political agendas. Given today's level of opinion-driven
programming disguised as journalism, the Society of Professional Journalists' code of ethics is surely worth a second look. But Soviet standards
were another matter. How would they have stacked up against the society's four guiding journalistic principles?

In Soviet times the state and the Communist Party tightly controlled
television, radio, and newspapers—a control that was enforced by the

Soviet penal code. Television and radio stations were governed by an arm of the party, the Committee for Television and Radio Broadcasting. Under the committee's guidance, all communications strictly adhered to a uniquely Soviet message. In so doing, they were essentially charged with carrying out two of the Communist Party's principal functions: spreading propaganda and controlling dissent. In the process all print and broadcast communications were subject to a government censorship agency known as Glavlit (Main Directorate for the Protection of State Secrets in the Press). In essence, censors were empowered to amend or block any media article that compromised state secrets, criticized Soviet ideology, or questioned government policies. As a result, Soviet journalism was characterized by strict control of the flow of information. There was no independent search for truth but, rather, a government-approved version of "alternate facts." The committee's strict adherence to Communist Party direction precluded any notion of independent journalism, and journalists were accountable not to the public but to their government overseers. To bring uncensored information into the Soviet Union, Western-based, Western-funded programs such as the VOA (Voice of America), Radio Free Europe, and the BBC (British Broadcasting Corporation) brought news from outside the Iron Curtain into the Soviet Bloc. Those efforts were met with concerted efforts by the Soviet government to jam their signals (much as Radio Free Europe / Radio Liberty has been subjected to similar countermeasures since Russia's 2022 invasion of Ukraine).

Subsidized by the state, print media was once considered the most influential media outlet, designed to be inexpensive and accessible to the masses, particularly the lesser-educated working class. Among the first print media established after the Bolshevik Revolution was *Pravda* (Truth), created to convey the newly formed Soviet communist government's message. Over the years most Soviet journalists and editors became members of the Russian Union of Journalists, an organization controlled by the Communist Party. Editors were put into place with the approval of the Communist Party, and journalists were trained at institutions established by the party. Following *Pravda*, other publications were established, each with its own specialty. One such entity was *Komsomolskaya Pravda*, a Communist Party publication geared toward young Soviets. But regardless of their target audience, all such publications operated under the auspices of the party, just as in the case of radio and television.

As the Soviet Union headed toward collapse, an emerging class of dedicated journalists crawled out from under the thumb of the Communist Party. As they did so, many newly empowered Soviet citizens began to break from quietly going about their business and looking the other way, as they'd been cowed into doing under communism. No longer subdued into silence, many embraced the freedom to openly discuss politics, question authority, and express disapproval of government policies. Fueled both by citizens' pent-up desire to voice their opinions and the growing journalistic freedoms later enshrined in the 1993 Russian constitution, Western-style, independent broadcast and print outlets were established. The most popular and influential broadcast and print outlets were as follows:

Echo of Moscow radio went on the air in 1990, guided by the principle that "all significant points of view should be presented."[2] Known for its independence, Echo of Moscow was part of a burgeoning empire known as Media Most, which was founded by Russian media tycoon Vladimir Gusinsky. Echo of Moscow's format was news and talk radio, with particular attention given to political and social issues. In August 1991 an emboldened Echo of Moscow went out on a limb by opposing the KGB-led coup against Gorbachev and, in so doing, invited an unsuccessful attempt by the KGB Alpha Team to cut off its broadcast. In the years to come, Echo of Moscow's broadcasts would continue to test the limits imposed by government watchdogs. In 2014 Echo of Moscow received a warning from Roskomnadzor—a modern-day Glavlit that the Russian government established to monitor, control, and censor mass media and the internet. What was Echo's offense? Its "unfavorable" coverage of the 2014 conflict between Ukrainian armed forces and Russia-friendly rebels in Eastern Ukraine.[3] At the time of that conflict, Russia was experiencing a rise in nationalism, leading to threats against Echo of Moscow and references to its editors as enemies of Russia. That sentiment ultimately contributed to Echo's takeover in 2018 by Gazprom, Russia's

Kremlin-friendly, majority state-owned, multibillion-dollar natural gas corporation.

Despite its takeover by Gazprom, Echo of Moscow continued as a voice of independence. However, that voice was silenced in March 2022 as the result of a series of charges against Echo by Russia's prosecutor general. Those charges included the assertion that Echo was encouraging protests against Russia's 2022 invasion of Ukraine and disseminating lies about Russia's military. The prosecutor general's attack continued, prompted by Echo's interview of Ukrainian journalists who described the horrors associated with the invasion. The final nail in Echo's coffin was the result of Echo's refusal to adhere to the Kremlin's sanitized version of the invasion as a "special military operation" (rather than an invasion or a war) and Echo's failure to blindly support the Kremlin narrative that Russia was justified in (heroically) "liberating" Ukraine from the "neo-Nazi, fascist drug addicts" who the Kremlin claimed had taken over the Ukrainian government.[4] Days later Echo of Moscow was forced off the air.

Novaya Gazeta was one of Russia's early independent print outlets. Founded in 1993, the publication was built, in part, with the support of Mikhail Gorbachev, who used a portion of the money earned from his 1990 Nobel Peace Prize for its founding. From its inception *Novaya Gazeta* had a reputation for hard-hitting investigative journalism and political commentary that was critical of the Russian military's brutal oppression in Chechnya, government corruption, and, later, Putin. In response, several *Novaya Gazeta* journalists and editors were assassinated, including Anna Politkovskaya, a journalist whose coverage of the two wars in Chechnya was critical of the savage brutality of Russian forces. On October 7, 2006 (Putin's birthday), Politkovskaya was shot four times outside of her Moscow apartment, once in the head. While shocking, that was just the last in a long line of attacks against Politkovskaya, who was poisoned in September 2004 while en route to a devastating terrorist takeover of a school in Russia's North Caucasus region. Her supervisor, the deputy editor of *Novaya Gazeta*, had earlier suffered a similar fate. In 2003 he, too, was poisoned, fell into a coma, and died.

Despite the inherent dangers of standing up for journalistic independence, *Novaya Gazeta* continued to operate. However, in March 2022, Dmitry Muratov, *Novaya Gazeta*'s Nobel Prize-winning editor in chief, warned that the publication was on the verge of being shut down due to a new law under consideration (and later passed) by the Russian parliament.[5] Said law would subject journalists to up to fifteen years in prison for spreading "fake" news about the 2022 Russian military invasion of Ukraine. In essence, the Kremlin defined "fake news" (or "false information") as any narrative that failed to align with the government's assertion that Russia's "special military operation" was neither an invasion nor a war, its claim that Ukraine was run by neo-Nazis, or that gave any criticism of the Russian military. As a result, the following day, *Novaya Gazeta* announced that it would remove all items referencing Russian military actions in Ukraine from its website and social networks.[6] Later, after receiving a warning about the nature of its reporting from the watchdog agency Roskomnadzor, *Novaya Gazeta* announced it would cease reporting until the conflict was over. In September 2022, following a separate complaint by Roskomnadzor, a Moscow court stripped *Novaya Gazeta* of its license to operate. Since then, an offshoot of *Novaya Gazeta* (*Novaya Gazeta Europe*) has been operating out of Western Europe. In June 2023 the Russian prosecutor general declared *Novaya Gazeta Europe* an undesirable organization, a designation that criminalizes sharing information from *Novaya Gazeta Europe* online and leaves its staff vulnerable to criminal prosecution in Russia.

NTV Television, like Echo of Moscow, was part of Media Most, the media-holding company built by Vladimir Gusinsky. With its opening broadcast in 1993, NTV's motto was "News is our profession." The station was staffed by respected journalists known for adhering to high journalistic standards. Broadcasts had a reputation for independence that drew wide-ranging audiences in Russia and other former Soviet republics, where viewers supported NTV's focus on politics and its willingness to criticize government officials.

In February 2000 (one month before the Russian presidential election), NTV began airing a series entitled *Kukli* (*Puppets*), a political satire that used puppets to ridicule high-profile Russian political figures. The puppet representing Putin was portrayed as a villain who was mistaken for a good guy but only because the other characters in the story were blind.[7] This generated loud objections from Putin's supporters, some of whom demanded that the show's creators be prosecuted criminally. Russians assumed that Putin would somehow retaliate. They were correct. On President Putin's second day in office, masked Russian Special Forces raided Media Most's corporate offices.

The pressure on NTV was a sign of things to come, a throwback to the type of journalism practiced during Soviet times. After the raid on his corporate offices, Gusinsky was arrested. After his release, Gusinsky fled Russia, but everywhere he went, he was subject to requests from the Russian government for his arrest and extradition. (An interesting side note—on the day Gusinsky left Moscow, he was accompanied to the airport by prominent Putin adversary Boris Nemtsov, who, years later, would be assassinated outside the walls of the Kremlin.) Gusinsky subsequently sold his interest in NTV allegedly in exchange for assurances that he would not be prosecuted.[8] Attacks on NTV and Gusinsky coincided with threats against Boris Berezovsky, who by then was a fellow media tycoon who was pressured to give up his ownership of another independent television station, Channel One. In April 2001 NTV was taken over by the Putin-friendly energy giant Gazprom. In 2002 the show *Kukli* was shut down for good. NTV's once-respected independent journalists were subsequently fired, and they eventually migrated to other media outlets. They, too, were shut down.

What precipitated these attacks on post-Soviet independent journalism? In the case of NTV, around the time that NTV was airing *Kukli*, tensions between Putin and NTV grew with NTV's exploration of a series of terrorist bombings in September 1999 that had targeted Russian civilians. Among the most devastating was an explosion that destroyed portions of a nine-story Moscow apartment building, killing over one hundred residents as they slept. That bomb, like others in September 1999, was set to explode at night, when it would inflict the most casualties. In all, over three hundred Russian citizens were killed during this series of bombings. Conversations with Russians I had befriended months earlier brought home the terror experienced by Russian citizens everywhere, who were afraid to go to bed at night, not knowing where or when the next nighttime attack would occur. The common theory was that Chechen separatists were to blame, which would soon light the fuse for renewed attacks by Russian troops in Chechnya. Following the apartment bombings, the Russian military brutally laid siege to Grozny, the largely Muslim capital of the Chechen Republic of Russia, attacks that ultimately left the city in ruins and led to the indiscriminate slaughter of thousands of civilians.

In her book *The Man without a Face*, independent Russian journalist Masha Gessen explores the September 1999 apartment bombings' nexus to Putin's first run for president.[9] According to Gessen, on March 24, 2000 (two days before the presidential election), NTV aired a program probing allegations that the FSB had a hand in the apartment bombings of the previous September, which some believed may have been a ruse to build Russian citizens' support for Putin's election and serve as a pretext to renew military attacks in Chechnya. NTV focused on events of September 22, 1999, when a local citizen in the city of Ryazan observed two people carrying heavy sacks taken from a car parked in front of a large apartment building. The witness also provided identifying information on the vehicle driven by the suspects. Given the apprehension stemming from earlier apartment bombings that month, MVD officers quickly responded and discovered three bags under a staircase in the building, each of which (according to the MVD) contained a powder that tested positive for the same substance used in earlier apartment bombings. Attached to the sacks were wires and a timer set for 5:30 a.m.—again, consistent with the recent bombings. Although it was dark and cold, the building's several hundred residents were evacuated and forced to remain outside for hours. The minister of internal affairs made a public statement regarding the MVD's initial findings, confirming that an explosive device had been discovered. To all, it was clear that a major catastrophe had been averted.

In her account of the events in Ryazan, Gessen states that, after the MVD went public with its findings (and as the MVD was presumably tracking down the identities of the individuals seen placing sacks inside the building), FSB chairman Nikolai Patrushev made a public statement contradicting that of the MVD. Patrushev claimed that the whole affair was merely an FSB training exercise, designed to test the public's vigilance. He claimed that the MVD bomb experts had erred, that the substance in the three sacks found in the building's basement was actually sugar. He also confirmed that the individuals who'd placed the sacks in the building were Moscow-based FSB officers, a curiosity since the head of the local FSB office in Ryazan denied knowing anything about the exercise. Refuting Patrushev's claims about "sugar," reporters from *Novaya Gazeta* located two young conscripts who had noticed an unusual taste to a substance they found in bags marked as sugar in a storage site used by Russian government agencies, including the FSB. The young soldiers' superior officer supported the assertion that the substance was the same explosive used in the earlier apartment bombings.

In its March 24 broadcast, NTV's investigation pointed to the suspicious timing of the September 1999 apartment bombings and the bombings' nexus to Putin's rise to power: it was soon after Putin's resignation as head of the FSB, just after he'd assumed the position of acting prime minister, and just as his 2000 presidential election campaign was taking shape. NTV's exploration of the theory that the FSB purposefully planted and detonated the bombs was dangerous. But what other evidence was there to believe the FSB had a role in the bombings? Enter Putin critic, whistleblower, and former FSB lieutenant colonel Alexander Litvinenko.

Litvinenko claimed to have had corroborating evidence in support of the theory that the FSB had a role in the apartment bombings. According to Gessen, Litvinenko also claimed that, as an FSB officer, he had been ordered to assassinate oligarch Boris Berezovsky (the former majority owner of TV Channel One) and kidnap prominent Russian businessmen. Soon after, Litvinenko was arrested by Russian authorities on charges based on his alleged use of excessive force. Although he was later acquitted, Litvinenko was subsequently charged with new crimes, prompting him to flee with his family to London, where he was granted asylum. On November 1, 2006, three weeks after the murder of *Novaya Gazeta* journalist Anna Politkovskaya, Litvinenko became seriously ill and was hospitalized in London. He subsequently fell into a coma and died on November 23. British investigators determined that the cause of Litvinenko's death was exposure to polonium-210, a radioactive substance produced in nuclear reactors. Traces of polonium-210 led to a radioactive trail that paralleled the movements of Andrei Lugavoy, a former KGB officer once assigned to the Russian Federal Protective Services, who'd had tea with Litvinenko in London just before he fell ill. Efforts by British investigators to interview Lugavoy and hold him accountable were unsuccessful, thwarted in part by Lugavoy's subsequent election to the Russian parliament, giving him immunity from prosecution and extradition. In September 2021, after reviewing the circumstances surrounding Litvinenko's murder, the European Court of Human Rights (ECHR) found Russia responsible for his death.[10]

Dozhd TV (TV Rain) was an independent, Moscow-based television station known for its willingness to stand up to the Kremlin. A relative newcomer to Russian journalism, TV Rain was established in 2010, its programming guided by the motto "Talk about important things with those who are important to us." Its format appealed to Russian-speaking youth, with its focus on news, documentaries, culture, politics, and business. Like Echo of Moscow and Novaya Gazeta, TV Rain was forced by Russian authorities to discontinue its Moscow broadcasts in March 2022, the result of its coverage of the 2022 Russian invasion of Ukraine. Its final Moscow broadcast was a less-than-subtle poke at Russia's government media overseer (Roskomnadzor), in which TV Rain staff's last words were "no war,"[11] followed by a recording of Swan Lake that mimicked Soviet television programming following the deaths of Soviet leaders and the August 1991 attempted coup against Mikhail Gorbachev.[12] Following its Moscow closure, Dozhd TV resumed broadcasting from a location in Western Europe. In July 2023 the Russian prosecutor general claimed that TV Rain "systematically violated (Russia's) media laws" and employed "foreign agents."[13] Like Novaya Gazeta, TV Rain was subsequently labeled an undesirable organization, leading to potential serious legal consequences for its staff.[14]

When all was said and done, Russia's brush with independent journalism was short-lived. Its decline began with Putin's election as president in 2000, followed by the arrest of Vladimir Gusinsky, the discontinuation of the program, *Kukli*, and NTV's takeover by Gazprom. Independent journalism's inevitable decline continued with threats and assassinations of *Novaya Gazeta* journalists in the 2000s. By 2012 the Russian government had assumed ownership and control of all six national television stations (including NTV and Channel One), whose real job is to take Putin's pulse and convey his beliefs to the millions of Russian citizens who get most of their news from television and the internet. In 2018 Echo of Moscow, too, was taken over by Gazprom.

The final nail in independent Russian journalism's coffin followed Russia's February 2022 invasion of Ukraine, leading to the shutdown of Echo of Moscow, *Novaya Gazeta*, TV Rain, and the relentless persecution of independent journalists throughout Russia. With the near extinction of independent journalism inside Russia, remnants of the Soviet propaganda machine are again in full control of the narrative. What is the result? Russian citizens have once again lost their voice—bullied into looking the other way, remaining silent, and quietly going about their business, just as they'd done in Soviet times. And what is one to think of independent journalism's exploration of the theory that the FSB played a role in the September 1999 apartment bombings and the murder of hundreds of innocent Russian civilians? Maybe it was a leap, maybe not. What about claims that Litvinenko and journalists such as Anna Politkovskaya were assassinated with a nod and a wink from Putin? It is not even a short hop.

When truths passed on by committed journalists are obstacles to an authoritarian's leadership, it helps to have high-profile surrogates to twist, distract, and hide those truths from view. Those stand-ins fill the void left by the demise of independent journalism with innuendo and alternate "facts" that are blindly accepted and passed on without confirmation by a legion of true believers, hungry to be told what to think. And so today's autocratic leaders employ trusted mouthpieces, enablers who cover their backs, spin their version of the truth, and use disinformation as a weapon.

A longtime soldier on the frontline of that effort is Russian television personality Dmitri Kiselyov, whose broadcast platforms include the popular television show *News of the Week*. Known for his ardent support of Putin, Kiselyov is an aggressive ultranationalist with a reputation for promoting conspiracy theories designed to arouse fear and direct anger at the "other." In the years preceding the 2022 Russian invasion of Ukraine, the heart of those conspiracies included allegations that Russians who took part in anti-Putin protests were "fascist puppets of the West."[15] That assertion was built on the theory that the West was bent on weakening Russia through US support of Ukrainian resistance to Russian incursions in Eastern Ukraine. Among Kiselyov's favorite targets are high-profile American political figures and events, dating back to his mockery of Barack Obama and Kiselyov's description of the 2016 US presidential election as the "dirtiest ever."[16] Kiselyov is also known for rants against homosexuals, which is exemplified by his assertion that their organs, rather than being donated to save lives, should be "buried in the ground or burned as unfit to prolong anyone's life."[17]

Moral tirades by Kiselyov, such as his attacks on homosexuality, are consistent with Putin's carefully crafted self-portrait as the defender of "traditional values"—an answer to what Putin describes as the West's "genderless and infertile" liberalism.[18] That assertion is one aspect of "Eurasianism," a Cold War-style worldview in which Russia is at the center of an expansionist empire whose principal enemy is the "Atlantic World," headed by the US.[19] Among the supporters of this ideology are far-right Russian intellectuals and the Russian Orthodox Church. With Kiselyov and others as his mouthpiece, Putin can parlay menacing attacks on Western liberal values into polishing his image as the guardian of moral conservatism. In the process Putin has built a close relationship with Patriarch Kirill, the head of the one-hundred-million-strong Russian Orthodox Church, who has assumed full-throated support of Putin. That support has included Patriarch Kirill's description of Russia's 2022 invasion of Ukraine as a "holy struggle" to protect Russia from "Western scourges like gay parades" and his proclamation that, for Russian soldiers fighting in Ukraine, dying "washes away all sins."[20]

In 2014, in a sign of the Kremlin's continuing drive to take control of Russia's media message, Putin appointed Kiselyov head of Russia Today (RT), a government-controlled global television news network built on the back of RIA Novosti, Russia's once-respected multilingual state news agency. According to the *Daily Beast*, RIA Novosti appears to have lost its respected status, having "committed the sin of neutral coverage" of anti-Putin protests.[21] In a 2020 Voice of America article, a former Echo of Moscow journalist lamented the growing atmosphere of intolerance of critical reporting in Russia. As a result, many independent Russian media outlets began reporting from posts outside of Russia to avoid laws that threatened to label them as undesirable organizations. One such law is the 2012 Foreign Agent Act, an echo of Soviet-era laws that were the backbone of Soviet propaganda and the war against dissent. Among the Foreign Agent Act's original targets were foreign-funded media outlets such as Voice of America and Radio Free Europe / Radio Liberty, although the law has since been expanded to strengthen the government's power over Russian-based mass media as well. Among the by-products of this law is the government's ability to effectively limit select outlets' access to advertising and frighten potential sources away from providing information to what the Russian government labels "undesirable" organizations.[22] But at their core, these laws are throwbacks to the glory days of the Soviet Union. And so in today's Soviet-minded media world, the rallying cry is fear—fear of dissent, disorder, and threats from external forces, a world in which only Putin, the strongman, can fix it.

From his position of power, Putin has at his disposal a surefire Soviet-style blueprint for suppressing the "enemies of the people," much of it patterned after an expression sometimes attributed to Josef Stalin: "Ideas are more powerful than guns. We would not let our enemies have guns. Why would we let them have ideas?"[23] His weapons include not only the media but the *siloviki* (Russia's powerful intelligence and law enforcement organizations), the FSB, the Investigative Committee, the MVD, and the Prosecutor General's Office—all backed up by the courts. With these tools controlling dissent is only a nod and a wink away. In such an environment, dissenters, critics, and/or political opponents have a habit of being imprisoned, exiled, poisoned, and/or assassinated. Aside from Politkovskaya and Litvinenko, other enemies of the people who found themselves on Putin's hit list include the following:

Boris Berezovsky was one of Russia's original oligarchs, a class of emerging wealthy business leaders who were among the many competing centers of power that Putin would later learn to manipulate in his quest to dominate the Russian Federation. Berezovsky initially built his fortune during the privatization of Russia's auto industry. In 1994 he was the target of an attempted assassination that appeared to have had links to his growing power. He went on to assume powerful roles in the Russian media and oil and airline industries, which would later open the door to legal problems in the 2000s. In the mid-1990s, Berezovsky assumed majority ownership of Channel One, a Russian television station with a reputation for reformist, anti-nationalist views. In the late 1990s, Berezovsky became an advisor to President Boris Yeltsin and, in that capacity, recommended that Yeltsin appoint Putin acting prime minister. At that time, Berezovsky supported Putin through Channel One and the formation of the Unity political party, which Berezovsky went on to represent in the Russian parliament.

Weeks after the 2000 presidential election, Berezovsky and Putin had a falling out that was sparked by Putin's plan to amend the Russian constitution, authorizing the Kremlin to dismiss popularly elected regional governors. Concerned that Putin was steering Russia toward authoritarianism, Berezovsky positioned himself in opposition to Putin.[24] In July 2000, two months after Putin assumed the presidency, Berezovsky resigned from parliament. From his Channel One platform, he launched attacks against Putin, leading Putin to declare that the Russian government would no longer tolerate attacks from a media run by oligarchs. In November 2000 the Prosecutor General's Office opened an investigation into Berezovsky based on his earlier dealings with Aeroflot Airlines. In late 2000 Berezovsky fled to London and, in 2001, sold his stake in Channel One, editorial control of which was then taken over by the Kremlin. While in exile, Berezovsky was convicted in absentia by a Russian court for an alleged fraud dating back to the 1990s. He was sentenced to thirteen years in prison but successfully fought requests for his extradition to Russia, claiming that the charges against him were politically motivated. Berezovsky died in London in 2013.

Mikhail Khodorkovsky was another of Russia's first successful businessmen whose roots included his role as economic advisor to Boris Yeltsin. Khodorkovsky built a fortune through control of Siberian oil fields, eventually leading to the establishment of Yukos Oil, Russia's first multinational corporation. In those early days, laws governing businesses were a work in progress, as were the allegedly questionable tactics by which Khodorkovsky and others built their financial empires. As in the case of Berezovsky, this would leave Khodorkovsky vulnerable to legal problems down the road. One of the original Russian oligarchs, Khodorkovsky was once thought to be the wealthiest man in Russia. As his profile and wealth grew, he spoke out against government corruption and eventually became one of Putin's loudest critics. As a Putin adversary, Khodorkovsky made financial contributions in support of Putin's political opposition.

Khodorkovsky was not the only oligarch to build his empire through allegedly questionable tactics, leaving him little sympathy from Russian citizens who resented the growth of wealth and privilege among powerful figures whom many viewed as thieves. But those who supported Putin stayed out of his crosshairs. This was not so for those who opposed him. In what was seen as retribution for taking on Putin, Khodorkovsky was arrested for fraud and tax evasion in October 2003. Yukos Oil's substantial assets were then frozen. In 2005 Khodorkovsky was found guilty and sentenced to nine years in prison, forced to serve his sentence at an isolated labor camp far from Moscow. While in prison, Khodorkovsky and his Yukos business partner were charged with new crimes: embezzlement and money laundering, resulting in years added to his prison sentence.

In the end the Russian government seized Yukos's assets, which were subsequently sold to Russia's largest state-owned oil company. In 2013 Putin pardoned Khodorkovsky, supposedly in return for Khodorkovsky's promise to stay out of Russian politics.[25] Upon his release from prison, Khodorkovsky moved to Europe, where he, like Berezovsky and Litvinenko, eventually settled in London in exile. From London Khodorkovsky resumed his attacks on Putin, stating that "only revolution" could bring positive changes to Russia.[26] The pressure mounted. Khodorkovsky's business partner was charged with murders related to Yukos's early takeover of oil production in Siberia. He was sentenced in absentia to life in prison. In 2015 the Investigative Committee of Russia filed murder charges against Khodorkovsky, alleging his role in the murder of a local political figure in 1998. Khodorkovsky remains in exile in London.

Yuri Shchekochikhin was a high-profile *Novaya Gazeta* journalist who exposed Russian organized crime's nexus to official corruption and explored allegations of human rights abuses in Chechnya. In 1995 Shchekochikhin was elected to the Russian parliament, representing the liberal democratic Yabloko Party. Like his NTV counterparts, Shchekochikhin explored the dangerous allegation that the FSB had staged the September 1999 apartment bombings to gin up political support for Putin and reignite the war in Chechnya. In 2003 one of Shchekochikhin's associates, who was looking into similar allegations, was assassinated. Shchekochikhin's scrutiny of the FSB included the assertion that persons affiliated with the FSB were laundering money through the Bank of New York, then under investigation by the FBI for activities linked to a massive Russian money-laundering scheme.[27] Shchekochikhin's investigation implicated a former high-level figure who once served under FSB chairman Nikolai Patrushev. In July 2003, as he was preparing for a trip to the US to meet with FBI agents about the FSB nexus to the Bank of New York, Shchekochikhin fell ill. He subsequently died of what appeared to be radioactive poisoning. Before his death Shchekochikhin published his final article for *Novaya Gazeta*, entitled "Are We Russia or the KGB of the Soviet Union?" The Prosecutor General's Office subsequently closed its investigation into Shchekochikhin's death without discovering his killer.

Sergei Magnitsky was an auditor for a Moscow-based law firm. Among the firm's influential Moscow-based clients was a successful asset management company founded by an American-born financier. In the course of his duties, Magnitsky claimed to have uncovered a conspiracy among members of organized crime, Russian government officials, and judges to unlawfully take over his client's asset management company. Rather than investigate those claims, Russian authorities charged Magnitsky with alleged crimes associated with his work as auditor for his American client. In 2008, while in jail awaiting trial, Magnitsky died—seven days prior to his mandatory release date. His death was said to have resulted from denial of medical treatment for illnesses including gallstones and pancreatitis. It was later determined that beatings Magnitsky suffered while in jail played a role in his death. In 2012 the US Congress passed the Magnitsky Act, denying Russian officials associated with Magnitsky's death entry into the US and access to US banking institutions.

Sergei Skripal was a former officer of the Russian GRU (The Main Directorate of the General Staff of the Armed Forces of the Russian Federation), the powerful intelligence arm of Russian Armed Forces, who clandestinely worked with British intelligence services starting in the late 1990s. Skripal was subsequently arrested by the FSB, convicted of high treason, and sentenced to thirteen years in a Russian prison. In 2010 he was released from prison following a prisoner exchange between the US and Russia in which several Russian spies, positioned in the US by the Russian SVR, were also released. From there Skripal moved to Salisbury, England, where he was granted British citizenship. In 2018, during a visit by his daughter to his Salisbury home, Skripal and his daughter were poisoned with novichok, a highly toxic nerve agent developed by the Soviet Union that, in minute amounts, can cause death. British investigators determined that the front doorknob of Skripal's home had been coated with novichok, which also caused some British police investigators to fall seriously ill. Skripal and his daughter were hospitalized in critical condition, but they recovered. Not long after, two British citizens fell seriously ill from novichok poisoning after handling a discarded perfume bottle they found in Skripal's neighborhood. One died. British authorities eventually traced Skripal's assassination attempt to two current GRU officers who, having been caught on surveillance camera in Skripal's neighborhood, claimed to have traveled to Salisbury as tourists. Those individuals, who are fully identified, remain in Russia, out of reach of British authorities. In September 2021 British authorities charged a third Russian for his role in the attempted assassination. Skripal has since left the UK.

Boris Nemtsov was a figure in Boris Yeltsin's presidential administration who helped bring about reforms in the Russian economy. A Putin critic, Nemtsov served as a member of the Russian parliament and, in 2008, founded a liberal democratic political movement that included other well-known Putin adversaries. A leading figure in the opposition against Putin, Nemtsov used his perch as opposition leader to directly challenge Putin, accusing his regime of being undemocratic, authoritarian, and corrupt. In the months following the 2014 Olympic games in Sochi, Russia, Nemtsov focused on claims of embezzlement of official funds that allegedly benefitted Putin and his inner circle. Nemtsov's profile grew considerably as he led demonstrations against voting fraud in Russian elections, which accounted for some of his many arrests.

Following the 2014 Maidan Revolution in Ukraine, which prompted Putin-friendly Ukrainian president Viktor Yanukovych to flee to Russia, Nemtsov stood in opposition to the involvement of Russian troops in the military conflict over disputed territory in Eastern Ukraine. He also declined to discount the allegation that a Russian surface-to-air missile had been launched from Eastern Ukraine by Russian-friendly forces, resulting in the downing of Malaysian Airlines flight 17 and the deaths of 298 civilians.[28] In February 2015 on a bridge overlooking the Kremlin, Nemtsov was assassinated. At the time of his death, he was reportedly preparing a document entitled "Putin. War," which focused on the involvement of Russian "little green men"—Russian army troops lacking military insignias who'd helped stage the Russian takeover of Ukrainian Crimea in 2014.[29]

Alexei Navalny is a Russian political activist whose principal focus has been corruption in the Putin administration. He coined the description of Russian leaders affiliated with Putin as the "party of crooks and thieves."[30] A reformer, Navalny is the embodiment of Solzhenitsyn's observation that "to stand up for truth is nothing! For truth you have to sit in jail."[31] Navalny has supported political parties opposed to Putin and has led numerous demonstrations targeting the wealth secretly built by Putin. In his documentary *Putin's Palace*, Navalny exposed details of a mansion allegedly built for Putin on the Black Sea at a cost of over $1 billion. Navalny has also been at the forefront of developing voting strategies to take parliamentary seats from Putin's United Russia political party. With his appeal to many younger supporters, Navalny has been closely followed in Russia and internationally through his postings on social media, including on YouTube and Twitter. As a result, Navalny has been the object of political retribution through physical attacks, poisoning, and arrests for criminal charges. In 2018 Navalny was barred from running for president against Putin based on a 2014 conviction for embezzlement for which he'd received a three-and-a-half-year suspended sentence.

In August 2020 Navalny fell seriously ill while on a flight from Tomsk, Russia, to Moscow. The cause of his illness was determined to be novichok, a nerve agent like that used in the assassination attempt on Sergei Skripal. (This was not the first physical attack against Navalny; a previous attacker threw a caustic chemical in his face, leading to partial blindness in his right eye.) An investigation by a team of Western and independent Russian investigative journalists pointed to the FSB's role in Navalny's poisoning. Investigators based their conclusion on their tracking of communications and travel by a special team of FSB officers who specialized in the use of chemical substances, who were determined to be in Navalny's vicinity just before he fell ill.[32] After some wrangling, Navalny was transferred to Berlin for medical treatment. In January 2021, following his partial recovery, Navalny voluntarily returned to Russia, fully aware that he would be arrested for violating the terms of his 2014 suspended sentence for embezzlement. What was the basis of his violation? His failure to report to the Russian federal prison service while being treated for novichok poisoning in Berlin. Navalny is currently imprisoned in a Russian labor colony following additional charges based on his work as an anti-Putin activist.

Vladimir Kara-Murza is a high-profile Moscow-based journalist, filmmaker, politician, and contributing columnist for the *Washington Post*. He is affiliated with Open Russia, a nongovernmental organization founded by Mikhail Khodorkovsky that is committed to building an independent media, political education, and rule of law and to supporting political prisoners. Like Navalny and so many others, Kara-Murza was twice the object of attempts to silence his efforts through poisoning, with each time leaving him in a coma.

A one-time protégé of Boris Nemtsov, Kara-Murza assumed a dangerous antiwar stance following the 2022 Russian invasion of Ukraine, having accused the Russian military of committing war crimes against Ukrainian civilians. Through his words he served as the voice of the multitudes of Russian citizens who painfully struggle with the invasion of a next-door neighbor, many of whom are repulsed by the war. Among the latter are those with close family ties to Ukraine and the hundreds of thousands who have fled Russia since the invasion. In so doing, they have lost their voice, their connection to friends and family, and their home. Following his remarks, Russian authorities arrested Kara-Murza for spreading "false information" based on "political hatred" (toward Russian authorities).[33] His arrest was also a clear warning to his many followers and would-be political dissidents. In April 2022 Kara-Murza was arrested on charges like those that led to the shutdown of Echo of Moscow, *Novaya Gazeta*, and TV Rain, in which persons convicted of spreading fake news about the war in Ukraine face up to fifteen years in prison.[34] The following September Kara-Murza was charged with treason, after which a trial was held behind closed doors. In April 2023 Kara-Murza was sentenced to twenty-five years in a Russian labor camp, the sentence having been imposed by one of the judges sanctioned by the US under the 2012 Magnitsky Act.

Maria Ovsyannikova is a journalist and former editor for Channel One, the popular state-supported Russian television station once owned by Boris Berezovsky. During a live Channel One broadcast in March 2022, Ovsyannikova shouted, "Stop the war. No war!" as she held up a sign that read, "Don't believe the propaganda. They're lying to you here."[35] The sign concluded with the following words (in English): "Russians against the war."[36] In a separate prerecorded video, Ovsyannikova made clear her shame for her work with Channel One and her role in spreading Kremlin "propaganda." During that video Ovsyannikova wore a necklace bearing the colors of both the Ukrainian and Russian flags. She placed the blame for the war on Vladimir Putin and encouraged Russians to protest the war.[37] In July 2022 Ovsyannikova did just that as she took a position near the Kremlin, holding a sign that read, "Putin is a killer. His soldiers are fascists."[38] Ovsyannikova was subsequently arrested and is facing ten years in prison on charges of spreading false information about the Russian army. In October 2022 Ovsyannikova fled Russia for an undisclosed European country.

These are only some of the high-profile instances of poisoning, assassination, exile, and imprisonment of influential Russian citizens who have crossed swords with Putin and/or the FSB. No doubt there are and will be many more, including the hundreds of thousands who have exposed themselves to arrest by taking a stand against the 2022 invasion of Ukraine. Among them are the online journalists forced to speak their minds from outside Russia, the thousands who have been jailed for expressing their opposition to the war, and the hundreds of thousands of draft-age men who have demonstrated their dissent by voting with their feet, refusing to die for a cause they don't believe in. In so doing, they have left behind their homes, their families, and careers for unfamiliar countries. But these Russian citizens are not the first to face Putin's wrath for challenging his image and authority. The FSB Alpha Team's response to crisis situations in the early 2000s were a sign of things to come, given their equally dark and unambiguous message to any person or group that took on Putin.

Like every SWAT operation involving hostages, teams such as the FSB Alpha Team are charged with addressing crisis situations that are inherently dangerous for everyone: the innocents, hostage takers, and operators (SWAT team members). The danger that someone might be seriously injured or killed is ever-present, and that "someone" is often the hostage takers, who are sometimes bent on ensuring their own deaths and taking innocents with them. As a SWAT operator of many years, I learned to appreciate the complexities of any operation. But my deeper appreciation stemmed from closely following crisis situations handled by the FBI's Hostage Rescue Team (HRT), a full-time, specially trained team of agents on call to respond to the most high-profile, complex, and dangerous missions. For HRT, like any professional law enforcement body, the only happy ending to any hostage crisis is bringing everyone out unharmed, especially the innocents and fellow operators. That is the nature of the beast. And that's why most professional assault teams, when time and circumstances allow, work together with fellow agents/officers specially trained in the delicate art of negotiation—behavioral science experts who are skilled at assessing what makes a hostage taker tick—in search of nonviolent pathways to defuse an ugly situation.

Unless there is an imminent threat to hostages, negotiators are generally not on the clock. Negotiations can go on for days and sometimes weeks, supplemented by tools to determine in real time what is taking place "in the room where it happens."[39] Developing strategies to defuse the situation and bring everyone out unharmed is the top priority. But whenever there is a possibility of harm, plans include stationing medical experts, ambulances, firefighters, or other emergency services nearby. If negotiations are unsuccessful, assault teams are prepared to take that landmine-laden step of aggressively taking control of an ugly situation. In short, when time permits, every step of every operation is carefully considered in advance. And whenever possible, the first steps reflect the preference for nonviolent options. When a violent assault is the only remaining option, plans are executed that employ only necessary force, guided by the use of weapons carefully chosen to minimize danger to innocents, by operators skilled in the precision use of those weapons. Having said that, I've seen that even the best-laid plans run up against chaotic or unforeseen circumstances, and the most any team can do is anticipate contingencies based on training, experience, and available intelligence. In the end, however the mission turns out, there is an immeasurable amount of second-guessing and step-by-step, slow-motion reconstruction that takes place after every confrontation. Each event is a lesson: How can we do this better next time? What did we do wrong? What did we do right? And in the darkest situations, that intense scrutiny, however painful, includes the press, government agencies, and the public.

That's the mindset that guided me as I coordinated best-practices training exchanges between HRT and the FSB's Alpha Team at the HRT training facility in Quantico, Virginia. The Russians clearly took that exchange seriously, as is evidenced by the fact that Russia's top general in charge of Alpha Team personally took part in all the drills and reciprocated by inviting HRT to train with Alpha Team in their Moscow-based facility. My enthusiasm for the exchange stemmed from my belief that HRT had a lot to offer due largely to its rigorous screening, extensive training, years of experience, commitment to excellence, and its own painful lessons learned. So it was my hope that, sandwiched between the inevitable guy talk about weapons and tactics, HRT might tease Alpha Team into taking a more professional, hostage-friendly approach to crisis situations. Where did I get the idea that Alpha Team's tactics were lacking? It was from my familiarity with Alpha Team's approach to putting out flames in Russian hotspots, where terrorists were sure to be systematically eliminated, sometimes at the cost in lives of hundreds of hostages. Two situations that exemplified Alpha Team's response to crisis situations took place in Moscow and Beslan, Russia, in the early 2000s:

Moscow theater crisis: On October 23, 2002, over fifty terrorists claiming to be members of the Chechen Army took over the Dubrovka Theater in Moscow, where over eight hundred unsuspecting guests had come to see a popular musical. The takeover began with one of the terrorists walking on stage and firing an automatic weapon toward the ceiling, demanding that Russian forces leave Chechnya. The FSB took charge, assuming responsibility for defusing the situation, ensuring the safe release of the hostages, and bringing the terrorists to justice.

The takeover lasted fifty-eight hours, during which many of the hostages were able to use cellphones to contact friends and relatives, pleading that the FSB end the crisis peacefully. Amid negotiations, the FSB developed a tactical plan: from passageways leading into the theater, they would pump in a gas that would cause everyone, terrorists and hostages alike, to fall asleep. In theory, according to the plan, all the hostages would then be rescued and the terrorists peacefully arrested. As negotiators were achieving some success in gaining the release of hostages, the FSB implemented their plan, forcing gas into the theater. As expected, everyone—hostages and hostage takers alike—fell asleep. In the immediate aftermath, government officials claimed that all the terrorists had been killed and that there were no casualties among the hostages. That claim proved to be far from accurate. In fact, 129 people, most of them hostages, died in the immediate aftermath of the operation. Where did things go wrong?

As Masha Gessen describes in *The Man without a Face*, although the use of gas went as planned, once brought out of the theater, many of the hostages, still asleep, were laid on their backs. Since no arrangements had been made to provide medical attention, many of them choked to death on their own vomit or were otherwise unable to breathe. Some of the hostages were loaded onto buses for transport to a hospital, several of whom choked to death in their seats as their heads tilted backward. Once hostages arrived at the hospital, the FSB refused to tell doctors what substance had been used to put everyone to sleep, thus precluding doctors from providing antidotes. As a result, some hostages slipped into comas and died. So what was the FSB doing while hostages were dying in their sleep? Photographs shown on Russian television confirmed that all the terrorists had been "shot dead, presumably when they were unconscious."[40]

There was never a credible official Russian investigation into the events of October 2002. No government official was ever officially held accountable for the hostages' demise or the point-blank execution of sleeping terrorists. One explanation for the death of hostages was that, to maintain the secrecy of its operation, the FSB had declined to station ambulances nearby or prepared to medically treat the hostages after exposure to the gas. Later President Putin awarded the FSB general in charge of the operation the prestigious Hero of Russia medal for his handling of the siege. On the other end of the spectrum was NTV; Putin objected to its unfavorable coverage of events that day, resulting in the firing of NTV's director general. Years later victims of the siege brought a lawsuit before the European Court of Human Rights, demanding a transparent investigation into the events of October 2002. The ECHR ultimately ruled in favor of the victims and ordered that the government of Russia pay restitution.

Beslan school: On September 1, 2004 (the first day of school), a school near Russia's North Caucasus in the city of Beslan was taken over by Chechen terrorists. Armed with automatic rifles, grenade launchers, and what appeared to be suicide vests, they demanded the withdrawal of Russian forces from Chechnya and independence for the Chechen Republic. For three days they held over eleven hundred people hostage, including over seven hundred children, most of whom were held in the school gymnasium. Clearly a nightmare scenario, this was a disaster waiting to happen, calling for delicate, deliberate negotiations and careful tactical planning to minimize harm to the hostages. After less than three days of negotiations, punctuated by intermittent outbursts of violence by terrorists against hostages, Russian forces stormed the school using tanks, armored personnel carriers, rocket-propelled grenades, and heavy machine guns.[41] In the end, over three hundred hostages were killed—more than 180 of whom were children. Also killed were over thirty hostage takers.

Most of the deaths took place on the third day, when Russian forces, led by the FSB's Alpha Team, launched an attack on the school. Eyewitness accounts and physical evidence suggested that the initial assault included Russian forces' use of a rocket-propelled incendiary device that struck the roof of the gymnasium, sparking a fire that caused the roof to collapse as the gymnasium was engulfed in flames.[42] During the ensuing exchange of gunfire between Russian forces and the terrorists, additional hostages were killed as they tried to escape. In the end, as in the Moscow theater takeover, it appeared that many of the over three hundred hostages who died had done so at the hands of FSB-led forces, suggesting that the FSB's primary mission was to send a brutal message to Chechen rebels, regardless of the cost in innocent lives.

The severity of the tragedy led to investigations by the Prosecutor General's Office and a commission composed of members of parliament, most of whom were members of Putin's United Russia political party. Although Putin ruled out a public inquiry, years later, another inquiry was conducted by the European Court of Human Rights, the result of a civil suit brought by survivors and relatives of the Beslan hostages. During the trial of a lone surviving terrorist, testimony by Russian government officials shed additional light on the facts surrounding the siege.

Given the chaos spanning those three days (and the lack of reporters on scene), there were several conflicting theories as to how the situation had evolved and who was responsible for the death of the hostages. In the end, the prosecutor general came to the unlikely conclusion that law enforcement authorities committed no errors during the siege. The United Russia-led parliamentary commission also declined to lay any blame for the tragedy on Russian forces, hanging their hat on the fact that the siege was instigated not by Russian forces but by the terrorists. Unsurprisingly, neither conclusion appears to be entirely accurate. For its part, the European Court of Human Rights confirmed, among other things, that Russian forces used heavy, military-style weapons during the siege.

Evidence was gathered based on eyewitness accounts, court testimony, follow-up investigations, and searches of nearby apartment buildings. Some of that evidence suggested that, as in the case of the Moscow theater attack, the FSB assault began amid promising negotiations. (Although, to be fair, those negotiations were taking place as spurts of violence were erupting in the school.) Evidence also suggested that, during its assault on the school, the FSB used weapons designed not to discriminate among targets but for use on the battlefield—certainly not for the precision strikes necessary to spare hostages. Evidence supported the claim that the FSB's initial assault was launched from nearby apartment buildings, had targeted the school gymnasium, and had employed weapons authorized by FSB Alpha Team leader, General Alexander Tikhonov.[43] One military tank commander confirmed Russian forces' use of tanks to fire antipersonnel explosives on orders from the FSB.[44] Witnesses also confirmed Russian forces' use of heavy machine guns fired from armored personnel carriers—accounts that were later supported by a Russian army general.[45] Empty shell casings found in nearby apartments confirmed the use of high-powered, rocket-propelled grenades directed at the school by Russian forces, which was an account later confirmed by the Russian government. Another factor that led to the death of numerous hostages was a lack of preparations to care for the wounded: very few ambulances and no firefighting equipment were on scene, despite the Russian forces' use of incendiary devices. To make matters worse, once firefighters had arrived (two hours later), many were unable to connect to water sources. In the end, the lone terrorist survivor was put on trial, during which many of the painful details of the crisis came to light. He was subsequently found guilty and sentenced to life in prison.

In the words of the German philosopher Friedrich Nietzsche, "that which does not kill me only makes me stronger."[46] With only two years under his belt as president, the Moscow theater siege could have been Putin's Waterloo. Instead, he managed to make the best of a very bad situation, no doubt thanks to some carefully calculated moves. By honoring the FSB general in charge of the response to the theater siege with the Hero of Russia medal, Putin signaled not only that his beloved FSB handled the situation admirably but that it successfully read the Kremlin tea leaves as to how he wanted the crisis resolved—an unmistakable message to future hostage takers. As for NTV's reading of the Kremlin tea leaves, they got a different message that was clear but painful: the media would pay a price for criticizing the FSB, ensuring that the facts surrounding the FSB's response to the crisis would never face public scrutiny. After Beslan, through its ability to steer the parliamentary commission charged with investigating the siege, the United Russia Party was able to ensure that no blame would be foisted upon government officials. The prosecutor general's conclusion that no one from the FSB was at fault for the carnage was another get-out-of-jail-free card for the government. And since no charges were brought against government officials, the courts played little role in holding government officials accountable.

When all was said and done, rather than weakening Putin, the sieges at the Moscow theater and Beslan school ended up strengthening his hand. His response to the attacks not only sent an unmistakable message to those who would challenge him in the moment (regardless of the cost to human lives), but it was a means of projecting Russia's power into the future. And if you believe anything about Putin, believe this: when confronting his enemies, he is ruthless, regardless of the cost in human lives; it is a cost he sees as a small price to pay for asserting himself as the leader destined to one day reestablish the glory of the former Soviet Union and rebuild the Russian Empire. As for accountability? As some bent on avoiding responsibility might say, "Admit nothing. Deny everything. Demand proof. And make counteraccusations."

CHAPTER 12

Those Who Vote Decide Nothing, Those Who Count the Vote Decide Everything[1]

Неважно, Как Проголосовали, Важно, Как Подсчитали

"Good government is good politics." That was the motto of Richard J. Daley—mayor of Chicago from 1955 until his death in 1976 and chairman of the Cook County Democratic Central Committee for twenty-three years, starting in 1953. As the former head of Chicago's highest elected office and its dominant political party, Daley is still considered the "most powerful local politician America has ever produced."[2] Each platform provided him with a unique perch from which to direct most aspects of local government. But good government alone doesn't guarantee reelection. It helps to have a foolproof system. In Chicago, Boss Daley built a well-oiled political machine—a big city, vote-generating juggernaut that gave him control of nearly all the levers of local power. As a bit player in that organization, who fancied himself a young intern in the Chicago school of power politics, I got a glimpse into how those with connections to the machine used political influence to their advantage (i.e., clout) and an appreciation for the meaning of the word *power* in power politics.

With his own unique brand of power politics, Putin has built a foolproof system by dusting off the Soviet playbook. In so doing, he has opened the door to remaining in control for as long as he chooses, as he simultaneously drives a stake in the heart of Russia's flirtation with democracy. And although it may be a stretch to compare Daley's leadership of Chicago to that of a modern-day former superpower whose territory spans eleven time zones, comparisons between Daley and Putin's style of governance highlight contrasting limitations on each leader's ability to exert control over their respective government institutions.

As political leaders, Daley and Putin had the same endgame: get elected and, once in power, stay elected. Both are/were Machiavellian leaders—cunning, charismatic, larger-than-life masters at steering elections in their favor. Both are/were empowered by diehard true believers. Both are/were able to effectively marginalize the power of their adversaries. And through an accumulation of raw power, both are/were ensured control of law enforcement as well as the legislative and judicial branches of their respective governments. In Putin's case, legislative supermajorities and control of the courts have allowed him to institute new laws and amendments to the Russian constitution that overwhelmingly favor his United Russia Party. Daley, too, was able to establish a form of one-party rule but was forced to deal with external obstacles that, unlike Putin, were out of his reach and kept him in check.

There were a lot of moving parts in the Daley machine. At its core was an army of patronage workers: street cleaners, park employees, building inspectors, city clerks, and more, whose government jobs depended on their loyalty to the machine, demonstrated by their eagerness to deliver votes and buy tickets to Democratic fundraisers.[3] Patronage workers answered to two bosses, both members of the same team: their employer and their Democratic precinct captain (often a city employee himself). The job of the latter was to acquaint himself not only with the city employees on his turf but with every voter in the neighborhood, to know which way they leaned and, using both carrots and sticks, lean on each to vote Democratic. Precinct captains made sure voters in their corner knew how to vote up and down the ticket. And what was most important? They made sure their voters showed up on Election Day.

Each precinct captain answered to his Democratic ward committeeman, who was in charge of one of the fifty political districts into which Chicago is divided. Ward committeemen took their direction from Daley and supplied precinct captains with their marching orders. They made sure that, in their fiefdom, the right voters were rewarded with favors and, in some cases, city jobs. Democratic voter turnout was their raison d'être. Their success allowed Daley to fill Chicago departments with reliable leaders who could be counted on to dispense return favors to the same people who'd helped put those leaders in power in the first place. And the beat went on.

Within the executive branch, Daley appointed the superintendent of police, whose most important qualification was his loyalty to Daley. Like much of Daley's administration, career advancement in the police department was partially built around favors. Police personnel with political connections could expect a boost to their career for doing favors for the machine—a system that worked to the disadvantage of hardworking cops who, whether by choice or circumstance, lacked a political "hook" (political benefactor) and were forced to rely solely on merit to build their careers. As for prosecutors, Daley alone had the power to greenlight his favored Democratic candidate for the office of Cook County's head prosecutor (state's attorney), who, if elected, was beholden to Daley when decisions were made as to who would and would *not* be pursued on state criminal charges such as official corruption. Daley appointed the head of the building department, whose inspectors decided what buildings and businesses were in compliance with city codes. Many of those determinations depended on whether owners were in the good graces of their ward committeeman. Daley's administration also ruled on zoning requests for new building projects, which were backed by investors who understood that having a hook in the seat of Chicago government (City Hall) was the first step in the approval process. Daley also appointed the heads of the Chicago Park District and the Department of Streets and Sanitation, both of which employed an army of patronage workers whose publicly funded side job was to keep Chicago's lakefront, parks, and streets clean and in good repair, especially in those wards that delivered the most votes.

Chicago's legislative branch was the city council, which was composed of elected officials (aldermen) who rubber-stamped Daley-approved legislation. Many aldermen were former precinct captains who'd demonstrated their loyalty as they worked their way up through the ranks of the Democratic Party. Their legislative qualifications started with a recommendation from their Democratic sponsor but also hinged on their track record for producing votes, raising funds, and their willingness to deliver on favors and look the other way when told. In their official capacity, they certainly did not present the type of threat that independent legislative bodies in other cities posed: no embarrassing investigative commissions or subpoenas of city employees. As for the small minority of independent-minded aldermen, it was not uncommon for Daley to direct his loyal supporters to turn off their microphones during city council meetings.

Cook County's judicial branch was also heavily influenced by the Daley machine. In a system in which circuit court judges were elected by popular vote, judicial candidates from the Democratic Party had to be personally approved by Daley. As such, the courts, especially in Chicago, were an extension of Daley's army of patronage workers. Candidates seeking the support of the Democratic Party had to be sponsored by their ward committeemen, who gave candidates the nod based on their proven loyalty to the party. In Chicago, if a judicial candidate was endorsed as a Daley-backed Democrat, his election (or retention) was generally a shoo-in, given the support of his Democratic sponsor and precinct captains. Once sworn in, elected judges ("full judges") were responsible for carefully considering legal arguments in criminal, civil, and traffic cases. But given their implicit debt to those who'd supported their election in the first place and the fact that they faced retention votes every six years, Democratic judges faced considerable pressure to give equal consideration to backdoor requests from the Democratic powers that be. Full judges also had the authority to appoint lower-level associate judges, most of whom were also chosen at Daley's behest. Along with judges, the Democratic Party controlled an army of court clerks, many of whom could be counted on to pass on requests from the fixers at city hall.

On the sidelines were well-heeled businessmen, bankers, and developers who were happy to invest in sure bets, knowing that their financial contributions and proven support of the party would help them get approval for their pet projects. Also on the sidelines were the low-profile but powerful Chicago mob bosses, who sometimes had a live-and-let-live relationship with Daley's machine. In some neighborhoods the mob had a lock on who got the nod for the job of ward committeeman, who was elected alderman, who got city and county jobs in their wards, and what businesses were awarded city contracts. And then there were the labor unions that worked together with city hall to make sure everyone got a piece of the booming construction pie that helped define Daley's tenure.

What was the endgame of this well-oiled machine? Getting the right people in power by getting out the Democratic vote. How he got out the vote of loyal Democrats was Daley's genius. Having been himself a former precinct captain, Daley understood that his biggest asset was his army of loyal precinct workers. As a buck private in that army following my senior year at the University of Illinois, I got an on-the-ground, real-world education through my firsthand exposure to Chicago politics—schooling that brought to life the meaning behind the book *Don't Make No Waves . . . Don't Back No Losers.*[4] After three years under the wing of my neighborhood precinct captain, I'd learned that favors were the currency used to cement access to power and that if someone did you a favor, you paid him back with two. I saw firsthand the loyalty demanded of Daley's patronage workers and the price for disloyalty. I came to appreciate the power of Election Day and the importance of simple acts, like driving an elderly widow to the polls. Along with other soldiers, I marched in Daley's annual St. Patrick's Day Parade, dutifully following the leader down Chicago streets as Daley blatantly flexed his political muscle. I watched Daley part the crowd like Moses at the Red Sea when he burst into a private gathering of party loyalists, and, along with thousands of others, I waited in an endless line in Daley's Bridgeport neighborhood on a freezing December night in 1976 to view his body and offer condolences to his family. As we passed his body, we said "goodbye" to a never-to-be-seen-again way of doing business that had been driven by Daley's army of true believers—a system in which candidates for state and national office, presidents included, often genuflected before him, knowing that he could make or break their candidacy.[5]

Despite his immense power, Daley had formidable adversaries. No, it was not the Republican Party, which, under Daley, was unable to get a foothold in Chicago. Nor was it the Independent Democrats, who'd openly called out Daley's shenanigans and the corruption among his cronies. Both were a nuisance but rarely a threat. His two antagonists, largely out of his reach, were the federal government (federal judges, federal prosecutors, and the FBI) and the news media (investigative journalists from newspapers, television, and radio), who exposed corruption and shined a light on the dark corners of machine politics. Chief among the latter was Mike Royko, a popular columnist with Chicago's powerful daily newspapers, who had a knack for pinpointing Daley's vulnerabilities and entertaining a loyal following in the process.

Investigations by the FBI and exposure by the media led to arrests stemming from the corruption and payoffs that fed the hidden side of the machine that Daley had built. On the receiving end of this one-two punch were the most egregious offenders: corrupt politicians, law enforcement officers, local Chicago judges, and clerks, not to mention City Hall fixers—the magicians with the power to make stacks of parking tickets and DUIs disappear—who whispered in the ears of machine-friendly judges to make sure the right people walked out of court barely bruised. As a result, Daley and his political heirs were forced to keep one eye on their rearview mirror as the FBI and the press gained ground. When they got close, it led to tales of corruption that publicly exposed the dark corners of machine politics, enraged voters, and infuriated Daley and those who followed in his footsteps. And when the FBI gained enough ground, Daley's cronies and those who'd carried on after his death ended up in federal prison. Did that happen in Putin's case? Not so much.

Putin is free from the headaches Daley lived with. With his unchallenged control of the FSB, police investigators, prosecutors, legislators, and the courts and with no threat from the state-controlled Russian media, his control of all internal government institutions is complete. Instead of fearing that he might end up on the sharp end of the stick, Putin is able to ensure that political challengers, pesky journalists, and other enemies of the "people" are the ones who end up in prison, exiled, or dead. And through a largely state-controlled media propaganda machine, he can spread his message and burnish his image at will, whether as a bare-chested horseback rider, a MIG fighter pilot, a scuba diver who miraculously unearths ancient artifacts at the bottom of the Black Sea, or as an ardent defender of the Russian Orthodox Church and its hardline ultraconservative values. Each well-publicized photo of Putin enhances the macho, larger-than-life image he works hard to cultivate. And from what mold was Putin cut that he would be inspired to recreate unchallenged leadership?

The Soviet Union was Putin's one-party role model. With one candidate on the ballot, Soviet elections never pretended to be democratic. The outcome was a foregone conclusion, given that the single candidate on the ballot had to be approved by the Communist Party. In a November 2020 article in *Russia Beyond*, the author opined that, although voters in Soviet times did not really believe their vote affected the outcome of elections, ironically, voter turnout was reputed to be near 100 percent. According to the author, that may have been due to a high level of state-controlled preelection advertising and the celebratory nature of Election Day, when goods normally in short supply were available to those who showed up to vote. For some, voting was an affirmation of voters' belief in the Soviet system and, therefore, a duty.[6] In the early 2000s, this was a way of thinking that was easily rekindled after Russia's flirtation with democracy in the 1990s. Once Putin came to power in early 2000, he put the brakes on democracy and steered Russia back to a modern-day version of Soviet-style elections.

In *The Man without a Face*, Masha Gessen, reporting from Moscow in the days surrounding the 2000 presidential election, described changes implemented by Putin soon after his presidential inauguration, changes that had all the earmarks of a blatant attempt to reshape the core of Russian democracy, maximize Putin's electability, and ensure the dominance of his political party. According to Gessen, Putin proposed legislation (later passed) that replaced elected members of the upper house of parliament (Federation Council) with representatives who were appointed by regional authorities, including governors. He implemented systematic changes in which those elected governors could be removed from office on suspicion of wrongdoing—without court intervention. In some regions he appointed presidential envoys to oversee the work of select governors. Local officials responsible for running elections focused on winning Putin's favor and essentially ceded control of election operations to the Putin-controlled federal government. By 2004 Putin's election commission had begun throwing out signatures of voters who supported opposition candidates, and there was evidence that prefilled ballots were sometimes delivered to psychiatric wards. For the opposition, getting their message out was another hurdle, given that Putin-friendly television stations were unwilling to advertise on their behalf and campaign venues were unwilling to host their events. As early as 2003, the Organization for Security and Cooperation in Europe (OSCE) questioned the democratic character of Russia's electoral process.

Over time, Putin engineered several changes in the law and the Russian constitution that benefitted both him and his party, United Russia. One such change was the power to harass and disenfranchise a segment of opposition political parties, ensuring that United Russia would face a diluted field of weak candidates. Ballot stuffing became a common tactic, as did accusations of "carousel voting"—busing voters from poll to poll. A large police presence on Election Day discouraged protesters who were angry about those changes, especially during the 2012 presidential election in which Putin had sought his return to presidential power. At some polling stations, poll watchers were chosen by United Russia, and poll watchers who contested United Russia's successes were ejected. After the 2014 invasion of Ukrainian Crimea by Russian troops, some Ukrainian citizens, particularly ethnic Russians sympathetic to Putin, were given the power to vote in Russian elections. And in many cases, votes were counted behind closed doors, limiting transparency. And how did Putin respond to claims of election impropriety? He immediately declared victory, thus cutting off election challenges before they could gain traction.

Despite having control of the levers of power, Putin has his challenges. Alexei Navalny, although sentenced to years in a Russian labor camp in 2021, is considered by many to be the most potent threat Putin has ever faced. Among Navalny's political platforms is his Anti-Corruption Foundation (FBK), which he has used to expose corruption in Putin's administration. As a result, the FBK was designated an extremist group and banned. But the modern-day dissident's efforts continued during the run-up to the September 2021 election in which all 450 seats of the lower house of parliament (the State Duma) were in play. Under the theory that many voters were willing to vote for anyone but Putin, Navalny developed Smart Voting, a means of identifying the strongest opposition candidate in each parliamentary district, regardless of their stance on issues. In theory, voters would be able to use Navalny's FBK website and an associated Smart Voting computer app to identify and cast their vote for the one opponent with the best chance of defeating United Russia's candidate. And how did the Kremlin respond? Days before the election, the federal agency in charge of monitoring Russia's internet shut down Navalny's FBK website and threatened Google and Apple with fines and prosecution if they did not remove the Smart Voting app from their app stores. Telegram, the most popular social media platform among Russian-speaking youth, subsequently followed suit after efforts were made to substitute its services for those of Google and Apple.

When all was said and done, United Russia ended up winning 72 percent of the 450 parliamentary seats. And what happened to Navalny? In late September 2021, as he sat in prison on charges dating back to 2014, the Russian Federation opened a new criminal case against him, exposing him to more time in prison. In March 2022, he was sentenced to an additional nine years in prison, having been found guilty of the ludicrous charge of defrauding his supporters and embezzling funds from his anti-corruption foundation. Since then, new charges of extremism were leveled against him in 2023, leading to an additional nineteen years added to his sentence. Harassment of the heads of his political movement also continued, including a raid in December 2021 at the homes of two leaders of his organization, the result of a Russian court's decision designating the FBK an "extremist" organization.

And so the Soviet beat goes on. Twenty-some years after assuming power, Putin has fulfilled his implicit promise to resurrect the Soviet Union. He has effectively crushed his opposition, taken control of the media, and commandeered the loyalty of the FSB, Russia's most powerful domestic security, law enforcement, and counterintelligence agency. In the process he has replaced Russia's early attempts at democracy with a foolproof system that allows him to control the levers of power unchallenged, with no opportunity for voters to pull his dance card on Election Day, no matter how outrageous or destructive his leadership. To be sure, instead of a system in which persuasion is the principal means of winning elections, Putin has engineered a blatant power grab in which the voting power of his opposition is watered down and votes of the party in power are artificially inflated. And unlike Richard J. Daley, he is not forced to cope with internal institutions that have the capacity to keep him in check: no out-of-reach law enforcement agencies, prosecutors, courts, or powerful journalists. What is the end result? The opposition becomes the enemy of the people, much of the populace blindly accepts what the media tells them, and newly voiceless voters lose the ability to impact their future, with little power to influence their leaders' decisions or stand up to their government's invasion of a next-door neighbor.

Elections obviously have consequences, not the least of which is the power to shape the future through legislation. And when the powers that be can dictate who can vote and how and what political parties are allowed on the ballot, you know the fix is in. In present-day Russia, as a result of his manipulations, the vast majority of legislators belong to Vladimir Putin's United Russia Party. Known as the Federal Assembly of Russia, Russia's legislative body is composed of two houses: The upper house of parliament (Federation Council) is made up of 170 *unelected,* regionally appointed senators. In 2022, 83 percent of those senators were members of United Russia. The lower house of parliament (the State Duma) is composed of 450 deputies, half of whom are directly elected by Russian voters; the other half are apportioned according to party. In 2022, 72 percent of those deputies were members of United Russia. Among the remaining deputies, some belong to parties that also support the Kremlin. Therefore, as the leader of United Russia, Putin effectively calls the shots as to what laws are passed and what amendments are enacted to the Russian constitution. Most changes are clearly designed to suit his political purposes, one of which was the 2020 constitutional amendment that enabled him to remain in power until 2036.

The constitutional amendment extending presidential term limits is only one instance in which Putin has used the power of the legislature to fulfill his political ambitions. In 2012, soon after Putin's return to the presidency, parliament passed the Foreign Agent Act, which initially targeted nongovernmental organizations, media outlets, and individuals engaged in political activity that received donations and/or support from outside Russia. According to the law, organizations that receive any foreign funding must register as a "foreign agent"—a term of art with sinister, Soviet-era undertones, implying that the organization is under the control of a hostile foreign government. Once so designated, those entities must adhere to a litany of onerous reporting rules.

Criticism of the Foreign Agent Act stems from its vague, overly broad language, allowing for legal interpretations that subject Putin's political opposition to criminal charges and imprisonment. A 2015 amendment to the Foreign Agent Act expanded the law, allowing the government to target foreign and international organizations designated by the prosecutor general as undesirable. The Foreign Agent Act was subsequently broadened, giving government the power to designate specific news organizations as foreign agents without explanation. In June 2022, months after Russia's invasion of Ukraine, parliament further tightened the screws on internal dissent by, once again, expanding the Foreign Agent Act. Under the 2022 amendment, any Russian citizen deemed to be under "foreign influence" can be labeled a foreign agent. The new legislation also prohibits persons so designated from teaching in Russia's roughly forty thousand public schools, organizing public events, and/or taking part in political activities.[7]

Under the Foreign Agent Act, individuals and entities targeted by the FSB have included independent Russian journalists and Russian language media outlets that were created to keep Russian citizens fully informed. Also targeted have been Western-based entities such as Radio Free Europe, Amnesty International, Transparency International, and Human Rights Watch. The law has also been used to target individuals such as Putin's nemeses Alexei Navalny, Vladimir Kara-Murza, and a Russian historian affiliated with the Moscow-based human rights organization Memorial International.[8] What was the historian's crime? The discovery of mass graves where victims of Stalin's atrocities were buried.[9]

Other laws designed to control dissent include Article 213 of the Russian penal code, which prohibits "planned disturbances of public disorder."[10] This vague law was used to prosecute Pussy Riot, an all-female punk rock band known for their use of "shock art" to protest the Russian police state. Best known for their unauthorized performance of "Mother of God, Cast Putin Out" at Moscow's Christ the Savior Cathedral, members of Pussy Riot were convicted and sentenced to two years in prison for their performance. More recently, parliament passed a law banning Russian authorities from enforcing rulings by the European Court of Human Rights, such as those stemming from lawsuits filed by relatives of victims of the Moscow theater and Beslan school sieges.

In 2016 the Russian legislature passed the Yarovaya antiterrorism law (named after a parliamentary deputy from the United Russia Party), which requires that Russian telecommunication providers store all communication data, including the content of voice calls, data, and text messages, for six months. The act further authorizes unfettered access to this information by the FSB, on demand, without a court order—a powerful tool that preempts the kind of independent judicial filter used in the West to keep law enforcement agencies in check. The act also restricts evangelist and missionary activities in Russia and, in so doing, indirectly protects the Russian Orthodox Church, one of Putin's most powerful political allies.

In early 2022, social media became one of the legislature's prime targets with the passage of a law directed at "foreign persons in the information and telecommunications network."[11] At its core, this law is focused on foreign tech and social media companies operating inside Russia, such as Google, Facebook (Meta), Apple, Twitter, and TikTok. Effective January 1, 2022, such companies were required to establish local, Russia-based legal entities that include a locally based, designated leader. In so doing, the law counteracts companies' attempts to minimize their physical presence in Russia, instead leaving them vulnerable to censorship and control by the Russian government.[12] Known as the landing law, this legislation is seen as a clear attempt to pressure Western-based tech companies to filter information seen as detrimental to Russian interests by threatening local company representatives with fines and arrest. In essence, the Russian government is forcing giant tech and social media companies to make difficult choices: police the content of their posts in favor of the Kremlin, risk arrest and being shut down, or voluntarily leave Russia altogether. In keeping with the spirit of this law, Russian authorities shut down Facebook operations inside Russia following the 2022 invasion of Ukraine, claiming it had engaged in "discrimination against Russian news media."[13] Shortly after, a Russian court ruled that the activities of Facebook and Instagram were "extremist."

In addition to the 2022 amendment to the Foreign Agent Act, the Russian invasion of Ukraine in February 2022 prompted another draconian censorship law designed to counter dissent by Russian citizens and information outlets. In March 2022, within days of the invasion (a term the law specifically prohibits), the Russian parliament passed a law imposing prison sentences of up to fifteen years for spreading "fake news" that discredits the Russian military.[14] The law was expanded days later to include "fake news" that discredits Russian government activities abroad. Using this law, the prosecutor general threatened to prosecute anyone who blamed the Russian military for atrocities such as those committed in the Ukrainian town of Bucha, where Ukrainian women were raped and civilians were executed by Russian soldiers, some with hands tied behind their backs. Among the law's principal targets are media outlets that fail to adhere to the Kremlin's characterization of the invasion as a "special military operation" as opposed to an invasion or a war. Included in the law is a requirement that journalists preclear their reporting of the conflict in Ukraine with the Kremlin. At the same time, Russia's media watchdog agency, Roskomnadzor, shut down access to foreign news websites such as the BBC for allegedly spreading false information about the war. As a result, in March 2022, most Western news outlets pulled out of Russia, leaving behind a chorus of Russian news outlets that were all dutifully singing in harmony to an alternate-facts hymnal composed by the Kremlin, designed to brainwash and dumb down the millions in Putin's orbit.

News outlets are not the only targets of the new censorship law. Soon after the 2022 invasion of Ukraine, Putin called forth the ghosts of Soviets past by invoking Russian society's need for "self-purification." This call to arms encourages citizen informants to report fellow citizens who refer to the war in terms other than a "special military operation" or who call for an end to the war. Much like the prefilled cards that Andropov's police distributed to the citizenry to anonymously identify those who violated Soviet norms, the Kremlin has modernized this call to action by encouraging use of the messaging app Telegram to anonymously identify the telephone numbers and email addresses of persons who contradict the Kremlin's "special military operation" narrative.[15] As the war in Ukraine continues and government fear of internal dissent has increased, the Kremlin has strengthened its ability to track dissenters through the development of increasingly sophisticated digital tools that are capable of circumventing encrypted apps, such as WhatsApp and Signal.

United Russia is not the only party responsible for laws that assert Soviet-style control over Russian citizens. Minority parties such as the far-right Liberal Democratic Party of Russia (LDPR) generally support the Kremlin. LDPR was established in 1991, having sprung from a Soviet-era collaboration between the Communist Party and the KGB. The terms *liberal* and *democratic* in the party's title are clearly misnomers. And with apologies to that emerging class of public servants throughout the world who are bent on selling white supremacy, religious bigotry, neo nonsense, deep-space conspiracy theories, I'm sorry to say, but these are not bold new frontiers. When it comes to rude, crude, and socially unacceptable, their Russian prototype is the former leader of LDPR, a shock jock politician by the name of Vladimir Zhirinovsky. With a reputation as a populist and showman, Zhirinovsky was a generally reliable political ally of the Kremlin until his death in April 2022.

Zhirinovsky was first elected to the lower house of the Russian parliament (the State Duma) in 1993. He held that office until his death in 2022, having served as its deputy chairman from 2000 to 2011. He was a lawyer by profession and earned a degree from Russia's prestigious Moscow State University. He had been a presidential candidate six times, starting in 1991, and at one time, was a credible candidate against Boris Yeltsin. As a campaigner, he was known for his uncivil debate style that at times morphed into chaos and over-the-top attacks directed at his debate opponents.

Born in Almaty in 1946, Zhirinovsky was the son of a Jewish father and ethnic Russian mother, although he reportedly did not discover his Jewish heritage until later in life. His father, whom he did not know, was a Zionist leader who fought for the establishment of Israel.[16] Some of Zhirinovsky's relatives were killed in the Holocaust, and many have strong ties to Israel. Despite his Jewish roots, Zhirinovsky identified as a Russian Orthodox Christian and, over the years, took extreme anti-Semitic stances, including a suggestion in 1996 that both the US and Russia find a place within their territories to "deport this troublesome tribe."[17] He also asserted his belief that Hitler's ideas were "not that bad."[18]

Zhirinovsky was an ultranationalist who called for the preservation of the white race, publicly abused women, and was known for violent outbursts directed at journalists who challenged his positions. He proposed denying Muslims entry into Russia, threatened to deport non-Russian minorities, and declared the need to build a wall around Russia. In one speech he suggested that Secretary of State Condoleezza Rice be subjected to brutal sexual violence at the hands of Russian troops.[19] When confronted by a pregnant female journalist with a question he found offensive, Zhirinovsky publicly suggested that she be violently raped by his aides. He threatened the use of extreme military force against Russia's enemies and, in one instance, following the downing of a Russian jet by a Turkish pilot, proposed detonating a nuclear weapon in the waters off Istanbul to drown millions of Turks. He advocated for the use of tactical nuclear weapons in Chechnya, endorsed forcible reoccupation of former Soviet Baltic republics, and suggested using them as a nuclear waste site. As a presidential candidate, Zhirinovsky promised that Russia would once again become a police state and would resume summary executions, and during his most recent campaign, he promised that he'd create a "brutal dictatorship."[20] With respect to Alexander Litvinenko, the former FSB officer and Putin critic, Zhirinovsky stated that traitors should be eliminated by any method. He subsequently supported Andrei Lugavoy, Litvinenko's suspected assassin, in his bid for election to parliament, thus ensuring his immunity from prosecution. In December 2021, months before his death, Zhirinovsky suggested that the Russian military bomb Ukraine on New Year's Eve.[21]

It is safe to assume that Zhirinovsky had an army of true believers. For almost three decades, he remained the leader of his political party and was reelected to the State Duma in every election since 1993. His buffoon-like behavior was renowned, as were his self-absorbed, vulgar statements. As someone who appeared to have an insatiable need for attention, he always found ways to force himself onto the world stage, seeming to feast on the reactions he got from racist, sexually offensive comments and anti-Muslim and anti-Semitic proposals and threats of extreme violence. His proclamations were a quantum leap from Khrushchev's "We will bury you" comment, which was shocking by the standards of its time. On the other side of the coin, one must ask, What mentality did it take to support this type of behavior over the span of twenty-eight years? Asked by a journalist why he supported Zhirinovsky, one prophetic voter replied, "Only a strong leader can save the situation in the country today."[22] That was 1994. That's the scary part—that he maintained the support of so many devoted followers, allowing him to remain the leader of a political party that plausibly contributed to the degradation of Russian society and was a blight on Russia's image on the world stage.

On any bad Russian day, I took great comfort in the words of a CIA pilot I met early in my overseas career. Prompted by a frustrating bureaucratic snafu, he offered these wise words: "Their country, their rules; you get to go home." For me, those were words to survive by. After years in and out of former Soviet Bloc countries, I had seen a lot. I became smug in the belief that Zhirinovsky's antics were uniquely Russian; he was just another eyesore on the Russian landscape, akin to the rundown trucks that belched rancid black smoke up and down Leninsky Prospekt with every change of gears. I was smug in the self-assured belief that Western democratic leaders were different, that despite personal weaknesses and/or widely differing political philosophies, they managed to conduct themselves in public within socially acceptable boundaries. In my view, they were bound by unwritten rules governing collegiality, with the goal of getting things done through cooperation and compromise, all in the national interest. From my main floor Moscow seat, it was obvious why Western democratic values prevailed over the Soviet Union's governing philosophy. And to me, it was a given that America's two-century-plus democracy was lightyears beyond the reckless absurdity regularly taking place on the Russian political stage. But that was then. Although it is unlikely that many Westerners have ever heard of Zhirinovsky, his brand of uncivil politics has become a prototype for a new brand of modern shock-jock politicians. And for me, the real shock is the fact that the once-unimaginable is now happening at home as we witness a watered-down version of Zhirinovsky's irreverence muscling its way into our national dialogue in a country whose democratic values and respect for human dignity prevailed some three decades ago over Soviet authoritarianism. Go figure!

CHAPTER 13

Control the Courts, Have the Last Word

In a nation built on the rule of law, independent courts have the final word. If you don't believe that, ask yourself why, in response to a unanimous Supreme Court ruling in *United States v. Nixon*, the most powerful man in the world defied every instinct in his bones by handing over damning evidence of his guilt, leading to his resignation from office and prison sentences for his closest confidants. In such a system, courts are the last line of defense—the great equalizer where impartial judges, guided by written laws, protect both the privileged and powerless from government abuse: illegal searches, seizures, invasions of privacy, and punishment without due process. Courtrooms are neutral territory where government prosecutors publicly present evidence of crimes on behalf of the people and where the accused demand the right to publicly defend against those accusations according to clearly defined rules. Civil courts are where we bring our grievances, fully expecting to be heard according to the laws of the land. It is also where we go when we feel those laws are not being properly executed and/or are beyond the boundaries of the Constitution. In every case, we expect to be heard by unbiased, fair-minded judges, who are experienced and well versed in the law and who ultimately answer only to the law and principles set out in the Constitution.

That is why the procedures for determining who is appointed to the bench and how cases are assigned to judges are so critical for maintaining our confidence in the courts and our democracy. In the US federal system, that is why judicial appointments have built-in safeguards against abuse of power, among the most important of which is the transparency that is part of the judicial selection process. Prior to their appointment by the president, federal judicial nominees are subject to rigorous background checks by the FBI and to scrutiny by a broad spectrum of public interest groups, the press, and elected US senators, a majority of whom must vote to approve nominees prior to their appointment.[1] Once they have crossed those demanding thresholds, federal judicial nominees are appointed by the president for life, a means of insulating them from political interference. Following their appointment, they can only be removed from office through a vote of impeachment by the US House of Representatives and a conviction in the US Senate. As sitting judges, they are subject to a demanding code of conduct, which was established in 1973, that guides them in the performance of their official duties, emphasizing concepts such as independence and impartiality. And like all federal employees, federal judges are subject to the Hatch Act, limiting their participation in partisan politics. Reviews of judicial decisions are also built into the US judicial system, leaving judges subject to potentially embarrassing reversals by appellate courts should they be seen as misinterpreting and/ or misapplying the law. In the end, we rightfully demand many things from judges: independence, intellectual honesty, fairness, impartiality, a thorough grasp of the law and the Constitution, and strict adherence to the legal principles that those documents demand. When all is said and done, it is their independence that allows federal judges to keep politicians out of the courtroom and maintain the confidence of the citizenry.

On paper, the Russian judicial system aspires to these same principles. The website of the Supreme Court of the Russian Federation outlines the principles governing Russian courts, stating in part, "Justice is administered only by the courts. Judicial power is *autonomous and acts independently from legislative and executive power*" (emphasis added). But saying so doesn't make it so, and the Russian Supreme Court's assertions of independence and autonomy don't hold water. To understand why the Russian judiciary fails to live up to this claim, it's important to begin with a basic understanding of its primary components.

The Prosecutor General's Office (PGO) prosecutes cases on behalf of the state and is considered by many to be the most powerful entity within the Russian judicial system. In theory, the prosecutor general is independent of the executive, legislative, and judicial branches of government. The prosecutor general is nominated by the president and appointed to a five-year term by the Federation Council, the appointed (*not elected*) upper house of parliament. All Russian prosecutors are subordinate to the prosecutor general.

The Constitutional Court of the Russian Federation is charged with determining the constitutionality of legislation at all levels of government. In so doing, the court decides whether federal laws and presidential decrees conform to the constitution. Constitutional Court justices are appointed to twelve-year terms by the Federation Council upon nomination by the president.

The Supreme Court is empowered to supervise the activities of all lower courts. Among the Supreme Court judges is a select group that is appointed to the Presidium of the Supreme Court, the final court of appeals. Like the Constitutional Court, justices of the Supreme Court are appointed by the Federation Council upon nomination by the president.

Ordinary courts are the basic building blocks of the Russian court system. They handle criminal, civil, and administrative cases, both nonmilitary and military. Judges of the ordinary courts are appointed for life by the president.

The means by which judicial candidates are screened and later appointed, promoted, and dismissed fly in the face of the Supreme Court's claims of judicial independence. Judicial candidates are initially screened by an official body known as the Judicial Qualification Collegia, which is composed of judges, representatives of the public, and one representative of the president.[2] In addition to its judicial screening function, once judicial candidates are appointed, the Judicial Qualification Collegia also has a voice in determining judicial promotions and dismissals. Despite having an inordinate level of influence over those functions, the process by which members of the Judicial Qualification Collegia themselves are selected is opaque, inviting questions as to its susceptibility to pressure from the executive branch. When all is said and done, the Supreme Court website fails to acknowledge how much power Putin and his party, United Russia, exercise over the screening, nomination, final selection, and retention of judges (and the prosecutor general), given Putin's role as the nominator and United Russia's final say in who gets appointed, thanks to United Russia's overwhelming dominance within the Federation Council.

The nature of the pool of potential judicial candidates is also at issue. According to Igor Slabykh, an attorney with law degrees from both the US and Russia, two-thirds of Russian judges are former court personnel who earned their law degrees online or through part-time study, suggesting a lower standard than might be expected of seasoned legal practitioners. Overall, there is little opportunity for attorneys in private practice to become judges, and many of the judicial vacancies not filled by former court personnel are filled by former officials from the Prosecutor General's Office and law enforcement agencies. It is therefore no surprise that the overwhelming majority of criminal cases (99 percent) are decided in favor of the government. This favorable slant toward the government invites a system in which legal procedures such as search warrants are susceptible to authorization based on flimsy evidence, allowing the government to harass opposition parties and to more effectively suppress dissent.[3] Lastly, although there is a jury system in Russia, literally one in a million cases are so decided, and as of 2008, defendants charged with crimes deemed as antistate (such as the cases against Alexei Navalny) no longer have the right to a trial by jury, thus eliminating an essential buffer against government abuse that is found in the US judicial system.

Having spent years in and out of federal courtrooms as an FBI agent and years in Chicago courts as a social worker, I have seen justice in many forms. I have testified in courtrooms that exuded an air of reverence for the law and in courtrooms that felt sleazy. In federal courts the professional standards demanded of us by judges were crystal clear, and woe be unto any FBI agent who was unprepared, fudged his testimony, or played with facts laid out in the four corners of a sworn affidavit. In those courts, although things didn't always go our way, we accepted the outcome, confident that each side had received a fair shake. In short, regardless of circumstances, there was never a question as to the integrity of the proceedings, which stemmed largely from the high standards of education, experience, character, and judgment demanded of sitting judges; the rigorous process leading to their appointment; and their insulation from political pressure.

My years as a social worker in the Chicago criminal courts in the late 1970s and early 1980s were another matter. In those days, although many well-respected, honest judges were able to keep systemic corruption at bay, their efforts were in stark contrast to other courts lacking that air of dignity. That was due, in part, to a system built on patronage, where those responsible for putting judges on the bench expected favors in return. One sure sign of corruption was the courtroom hustlers—unscrupulous defense attorneys who, day after day, lurked outside of our offices in crowded hallways in search of vulnerable criminal defendants in need of legal representation. Those grifters knew which judges were "on the take," or amenable to favoring them (for a price) over honest attorneys when it came time to assign defendants a lawyer. They operated with the tacit approval of the judges who demanded a piece of the pie for granting them preferential treatment and favorable rulings, regardless of the law. In some cases, those attorneys passed cash envelopes to judges through law enforcement officers and court clerks, who served as their bagmen. In so doing, courtroom hustlers were little more than carnival barkers, shilling for the man in the middle of the merry-go-round (the judge), where passengers fresh out of handcuffs paid not to get on but to get off.[4]

In the early 1980s, those acts of bribery and corruption drew the attention of federal prosecutors and the FBI. Thus began Operation Greylord, a wide-ranging FBI undercover operation that resulted in federal-bribery and corruption convictions of dozens of attorneys, court clerks, law enforcement officers, and local judges, many of whom my fellow social workers and I had appeared before on a daily basis. And how did the fifteen Cook County judges convicted in Operation Greylord get their seats on the bench? It was certainly not based on their honesty, sense of fairness, and impartiality and respect for the rule of law. Instead, many got (or kept) their jobs based on their loyalty to the man and the party in power. Like Putin's Russia, they were the product of a system that, in some cases, supported judges based on their willingness to pick up the phone when a fixer called in a favor. Nor were they hired for their dedication to the law, but rather their dedication to themselves and the people who put them in power in the first place. "Go along to get along"—that was their philosophy, or as my favorite newspaper columnist (Mike Royko) used to say, "Ubi est mea?" (Latin for "Where's mine?").

In Russia, rather than submit to the courts as Richard Nixon did in 1974, Putin is able to use prosecutors and the courts for his own purposes.[5] That power springs from his ability to shape the judiciary to his liking by drawing from a favorable pool of judicial candidates and manipulating the judicial selection and retention process. The result is a nation not bound by the rule of law but by the dictates of an autocratic leader and the political party he controls, resulting in a corrupt system in which the courts become a disciplinary arm of the presidential administration. What in theory should be an independent judiciary that protects citizens from abuse by government officials becomes an instrument to suppress and control dissent. If anyone has any doubt about that, just ask Alexei Navalny, Vladimir Kara-Murza, Maria Ovsyannikova, or the millions of thoughtful and compassionate Russians cowed into expressing their dissent in whispers, much like their Soviet ancestors.

As an autocrat with undisputed power and no identifiable, near-term end to his rule in sight, Putin is living the dream.[6] Having repeatedly manipulated the Russian legal system, he has been able to deflect electoral threats to his power and is supported by a rubber-stamp legislature and judicial system that he controls. By having manipulated the law and the ballot box since the beginning of his rise to power, he is assured that he will face only ineffectual challengers. He does not have to demand loyalty from those in his administration; it is a given. Control of his loyal FSB is by far one of his strongest levers of power, which he uses to control, crush, and eliminate his enemies. Having successfully vilified segments of the media as his enemies and rewarded those who support him, he has managed to control most of the narrative. And with his intrusions into social media and recent laws threatening imprisonment for spreading what the Kremlin deems to be fake news, he has closed the loop. So what's left? How about rewriting history!

"Dwell on the past and you'll lose an eye. Forget the past and you'll lose both eyes" (Кто старое помянет, тому глаз вон; а кто забудет, тому оба вон) is Russia's answer to "Those who cannot remember the past are condemned to repeat it."[7] That was likely the thinking of the Russian citizens who established Russia's leading human rights organization, Memorial International. Based in Moscow and founded by individuals including Andrei Sakharov, the renowned Soviet nuclear physicist, Nobel Prize winner, and dissident forced into internal exile in the 1980s, Memorial International chronicled Soviet repression and memorialized the millions of citizens who perished in Stalin's labor camps. In so doing, Memorial held an annual ceremony known as Return of the Names near the FSB's Lubyanka headquarters. Over a period of thirty-five years, Memorial archived the names of three million such victims—an estimated one-quarter of the total of those who died in Stalin's camps.

In December 2021 the so-called autonomous Supreme Court of Russia, the same court whose website boasts of its authority to act "independently from legislative and executive power,"[8] ordered the closure of Memorial International. The decision was seen by many as another in a series of attempts to redefine history and tighten the noose on openness.[9] The order was based, in part, on the prosecutor general's assertion that Memorial International was attempting to portray the Soviet Union as a terrorist organization. According to the *New York Times*, this was another step in the Kremlin's effort to aggressively remove "alternative interpretations of Russian history by organizations it (the Kremlin) does not control."[10] In so doing, closing Memorial International helped Russians shift their focus to "foreign foes instead of crimes committed by homegrown dictators."[11] In a related article, the *New York Times* reported that the day following the closure of Memorial International, the Moscow City Court ordered the closure of Memorial International's Human Rights Center, a separate but related office that maintained a list of roughly four hundred political prisoners then serving sentences in Russia. Following its closure, Memorial International was one of three winners of the 2022 Nobel Peace Prize, "based on the notion that confronting past crimes is essential to preventing new ones."[12]

But redefining the past is only half the story, as Putin took another page from Soviet history to plan Russia's future.

Under the belief that Soviet youth were destined to build a socialist future under communism, the Communist Party built social structures to ensure young Soviets' adherence to communist principles. Starting with children at age seven and continuing throughout childhood, those organizations injected themselves into Soviet family life, stressing the importance of loyalty to party principles above all. As a result, youth organizations flourished throughout Soviet history, especially during and after the Great Patriotic War, when Soviet youth were glorified for their heroic sacrifices in defending the Soviet Union against Nazi invaders. Communist youth organizations went on to thrive until the collapse of the Soviet Union, at which time they were disbanded. The three stages of Soviet youth indoctrination that later became a template for modern-day Russian youth groups are described below:

Little Octobrists (Oktyabryata) was an organization that Soviet children routinely joined at age seven. The name was a reference to Soviet children born in 1917, the year of the Great October Socialist Revolution (also known as Red October), when Vladimir Lenin's Bolshevik Party led the armed revolt that ended tsarist rule in Russia. Little Octobrists' uniform included a five-pointed star depicting a photo of Lenin as a child. Soviet children's participation in games and other social activities was their introduction to socialist ways of thinking and interacting.

Young Pioneers was the next stage of communist indoctrination, which began at age nine. Originally named the Vladimir Lenin All Union Pioneer Organization, the Young Pioneers was formed in 1922 by the Communist Party. In theory, joining the Young Pioneers was voluntary, although social pressure ensured that almost all Soviet children joined the organization. Their uniform consisted of a white shirt and red neckerchief. Young Pioneers attended summer camps where they were taught life skills, learned to be good citizens, participated in sports, and were taught the motto "Always prepared." Learning communist values was an important element of their training, including how to fight the enemies of socialism. During the Great Patriotic War, Young Pioneers aided the war effort by working on farms and collecting scrap metal, while some Young Pioneers joined the resistance during the German occupation of what is now Ukraine. The latter became popular heroes of a postwar Soviet film industry that glorified the bravery and sacrifices of Soviet youth.

Komsomol—the Communist Youth League—was the final stage of Soviet youth indoctrination. Established in 1918, Komsomol was originally known as the All Union Leninist Communist Union of Youth. Open to young teens at the age of fourteen, Komsomol posited that joining was voluntary, although, like the other youth organizations, there was considerable social pressure to do so. By joining Komsomol, members took the final step toward declaring their loyalty and desire to become members of the Communist Party, which was considered a step toward a respectable career. Komsomol activities included sports, drama, volunteering, and political work. Members refuted religion, drinking, and other activities that were considered distractions from leading a utopian life under communism and were subject to purges from their ranks if they did not adhere to the highest communist ideals. Komsomol membership increased significantly under Stalin and later reached its peak in the 1970s, when it boasted tens of millions of members.

Like the Communist Party, Komsomol and the other Soviet youth organizations were disbanded in late 1991. But in a never-ending quest to create new centers of power that he could mold and shape to his liking, Putin oversaw the reincarnation of Soviet youth organizations that began during his first term as president.

Nashi, a Soviet-style youth organization, was formed in March 2005. Roughly patterned after Komsomol, Nashi ("Ours") was a largely working-class, nationalist patriotic movement that claimed to be antifascist and antioligarch. Most members were young Russians in their late teens and twenties who identified as Russia's first post-Soviet generation. Supported by the Putin administration, Nashi's manifesto was based on the writings of a Putin political advisor. Political demonstrations by Nashi members were a means of focusing Kremlin dissatisfaction on recent global developments—in particular, the prodemocracy "color revolutions" that had recently toppled pro-Russian governments in nearby Georgia (Rose Revolution, 2003), Ukraine (Orange Revolution, 2004), and Kyrgyzstan (Tulip Revolution, 2005), all of which Putin claimed were backed by Western governments.[13] Members of Nashi saw themselves as "Putin's generation" and credited him with bringing modernization and stability to Russia. They promoted the notion of Russian global leadership in the twenty-first century and, in so doing, encouraged anti-European and anti-American sentiments. Sources of funding for Nashi included pro-Putin entities such as Gazprom, Russia's majority state-owned energy giant. With its strong pro-Kremlin orientation and its mission to stifle Putin's opposition, Nashi was referred to by some as "Putinjugend," an unflattering reference to the Hitler youth movement.

An article in London's *Guardian* newspaper examined Nashi's use of bloggers and internet trolls to support Putin's programs and vilify his critics. In a sign of things to come, Nashi communications, allegedly uncovered through email hacks by the group "Anonymous," suggested that Nashi paid hundreds of thousands of dollars to online trolls to spread information about Nashi recruiting camps and discredit Putin's opposition.[14] Examples of the latter included Nashi's use of social media to dislike anti-Kremlin YouTube videos, post unflattering responses to anti-Putin stories, and smear Putin opposition leader Alexei Navalny.

At its peak in 2007, Nashi had over one hundred thousand members, whose focus included training, political activities, and volunteering, including assistance to orphanages and restoration of churches and war monuments.[15] Nashi leaders organized retreats and summer camps, including mass gatherings at a camp outside of Moscow, where Nashi's Ideological Department recruited new members and screened applicants for their knowledge of Putin's positive accomplishments. Camp activities included two weeks of sports, political indoctrination, and paramilitary training. Nashi's political activities included harassment of Putin opposition groups and demonstrations against foreign leaders who opposed Putin's foreign policies. Unlike opposition demonstrations, Nashi rallies were authorized and supported by the Kremlin. Nashi political activities led to the creation of a political wing of Putin's United Russia Party known as the Young Guard. But with Putin's return to the presidency in 2012, Nashi began to fade, one of its last (and largest) political demonstrations having taken place on March 5, 2012, the day after the presidential election.

Network picked up where Nashi left off. Considered an answer to prodemocracy, fair-election, anti-Putin demonstrators known as the Bolotnaya generation, who staged gatherings in Moscow's Bolotnaya

Square from 2011 to 2013, Network was built around newly emerging issues, such as the 2014 armed takeover of Ukrainian Crimea by Russian forces. Largely composed of middle-class, educated young professionals (young Putin intelligentsia), Network was known for its pro-Putin children's books, counterdemonstrations against Putin opposition, pro-Putin street murals, and collecting supplies in support of pro-Russian separatists fighting Ukrainian government forces in Eastern Ukraine.[16]

Stopkham (Stop Rudeness) was another Nashi offshoot. Established by an ardent Putin admirer and former high-ranking Nashi member who'd received financial support from the Kremlin, Stopkham began operating in 2013. Its purpose was to expose lawlessness and the sense of privilege that was rampant on Moscow streets. Using public confrontations and YouTube videos, Stopkham attempted to shame those who flaunted traffic and parking laws. In time, however, Stopkham stepped on too many powerful toes and, to some, began to sound like the opposition groups its creator once fought. As a result, Stopkham lost the financial support of the Kremlin in 2016.[17]

The Youth Army Movement is the Russian Federation's latest Soviet-style youth indoctrination program. Formally established by presidential decree in October 2015, the movement is guided by the motto "For the glory of the Fatherland!" With echoes of the heroics attributed to the Young Pioneers during the Great Patriotic War, the Youth Army Movement's mission is to instill patriotism in Russian youth and, through military training, to prepare Russian children to defend against enemies along the Russia border (especially Ukraine), which are allegedly being groomed by the US and NATO as staging areas for future attacks against Mother Russia. In a *New York Times* article entitled "How the Kremlin Is Militarizing Russian Society," the authors describe the Kremlin's investment of tens of millions of dollars to enlist hundreds of thousands of children as young as eight into the movement.[18] The authors also link training events associated with the movement to the founder of Vympel, a paramilitary arm of the FSB also known as Directorate "V." In the weeks preceding Russia's 2022 invasion of Ukraine, large murals depicting young, uniformed trainees dedicated to defending Mother

Russia were posted on Moscow streets. At the time of the invasion, the Youth Army Movement boasted over one million members.

In the months following Russia's 2022 invasion of Ukraine, Russian authorities publicly complained of the failure of Russian school teachers (government employees) to instill a state-approved ideology in Russian children.[19] As a result, in July 2022, the Kremlin took the Youth Army concept a step further by codifying Russian youths' patriotic education into law. Since September 2022, under a mandatory program implemented by the Russian Ministry of Education and Science, Russian children in grades one through eleven have been required to attend weekly classes entitled Important Conversations, which are focused on traditional values and Russia's "rebirth." Classes include footage of the war in Ukraine narrated by Russian propagandists, portrayals attesting to the need for Russia's "special military operation," and lectures by Russian soldiers who offer positive interpretations of their actions during the war. And in September 2023, the Russian government issued new school textbooks that redefined post–World War II Russian history, asserted Russia's alternate-facts version of the war in Ukraine, and drastically toned down atrocities committed under Stalin.

As in Soviet times, political indoctrination of today's youth is yet another tool in Putin's modern-day toolbox, used to guide and control young people's thinking as they step into the future. And what will that future look like? Will Russian children ever learn the truth behind the brutal, merciless attacks initiated in the name of a Kremlin-crafted noble cause to "liberate" Ukraine from the "fascists" who were supposedly threatening Russia with invasion? Will they ever learn the whole story behind the blood-stained rubble that was once a Ukrainian kindergarten, maternity hospital, or a family's home? Will they someday be allowed to objectively evaluate for themselves the evidence of atrocities committed by Russian soldiers in Bucha in the name of protecting the Fatherland?[20] Or, like their Soviet grandparents, will they live in an Orwellian world where "war is peace, freedom is slavery, and ignorance is strength,"[21] a world subject to rigid censorship, where fact-based, open debate is nonexistent, the Kremlin defines what is real, and challenging government messaging leads to imprisonment or worse? With the Kremlin in control of the FSB, the media, the Internet, parliament, and the judiciary, it is increasingly difficult to believe the answers to these questions will ever favor an open dialogue as Russian youth enter adulthood.

These are the kinds of questions I would love to debate with the one FSB official I might have otherwise befriended had it not been taboo to do so—a man with an insider's view of the FSB, a unique perspective on modern Russian politics, and a family man with a huge stake in Russia's future. Unfortunately, that discussion will never come to pass.

CHAPTER 14

Afterthoughts and Aftershocks

On the walls of the San Francisco FBI office hung a poster that read, "Countries don't have friends; countries have interests." Although I passed by that poster almost every day for years, the message held little meaning for me until my second Moscow assignment. That's when I learned to appreciate the complexity behind that seemingly simple statement. With its implied warning against getting too close to the "other," as well as its importance as a professional survival tool in Moscow, those words became my personal "survival rule no. 1."

Colonel Viktor Gennadyevich[1] was an FSB liaison to the legat office. His job was to coordinate with my office on all matters of mutual interest. When we had requests of the FSB, we took them to Viktor. When the FSB had official requests of us, Viktor brought them to us.[2] And if something was particularly important, we could always count on Viktor to do his best. He was my ever-reliable partner in coordinating a series of best-practices terrorism training exchanges with the FSB and the person with whom I shared a sense of accomplishment and relief when, after the training, everyone returned to their corners. Viktor was the consummate professional. Under different circumstances, he could have also been a friend. But these were not different circumstances, and because we were on opposite sides of a decades-long, deadly game of spy vs. spy, neither of us could ever imagine a world in which we would cross that invisible yet unmistakably bright line. Instead, we were otherwise natural adversaries who comfortably shared a narrow strip of neutral territory and a common purpose.

Viktor was younger than me, a good person and a loyal FSB officer. He had an easy smile, a nonthreatening demeanor, and he immediately reminded me of the Russians whose company I'd enjoyed so much during my first Moscow experience in 1998. He spoke comfortably about his family, and I had no doubt he was a good husband and father. But of course, meeting his family was never an option. He had a great sense of humor, and we could joke about anything, including borderline taboo subjects, such as a well-publicized spy operation, foiled by the FSB, in which a British agent was allegedly caught communicating with a fake rock in a Moscow park.[3] We could also joke about the FSB's unwelcome intrusions into my personal life and how amusing it might be to listen to FSB recordings of my personal conversations years down the road. (One hundred percent loyal to the FSB, Viktor never acknowledged such intrusions.)

Viktor was my go-to guy at official functions: semi-formal gatherings at the US Ambassador's Spaso House residence, meetings between the FBI and FSB at FBIHQ, and painfully dry FSB conferences, seemingly designed to test the theory that a human being could actually die from boredom. But our differing worldviews burst into view during the 2006 Fourth of July celebration at US Ambassador Burns's Spaso House residence when Viktor and a group of high-ranking FSB generals grumbled and melted into the crowd at the sight of an approaching Mikhail Gorbachev. (As they did, I strategically positioned myself to shake Gorbachev's hand.) To me, our widely divergent reactions to Gorbachev epitomized the Grand Canyon divide between our worldviews: one side saw him as a visionary who, in partnership with Ronald Reagan, had engineered a peaceful end to the Cold War and opened new doors to Soviet citizens; the other side saw him as the man who single-handedly kneecapped the Soviet Union, leaving its citizens vulnerable to the threat of NATO expansion.

After a trip to the FBIHQ gift shop, I picked up a small gift for Viktor's son—a stuffed bear dressed in an FBI sweater. He laughed, thinking that I was trying to send him a subliminal message about recruiting his child as a future spy. Actually, I never thought of it. It was just a stuffed bear with an FBI sweater. In fact, we occasionally exchanged gifts with our FSB colleagues but, of course, within professional boundaries. During the holidays Viktor and his superiors always presented us with decorative bottles of vodka, and we always returned the thought with gifts bearing the FBI seal and bottles of American whiskey. But my most valued gift was a photo of me seated at Yuri Andropov's Lubyanka desk with his telephone pressed against my ear as I wondered how many times that phone had been used to launch operations against American intelligence or order the assassination of KGB traitors. At the time, I also wondered whether anyone paid a price for an act of generosity that might also have been seen as an act of friendship. But looking back, I clearly see that the "gift" passed to me in full view of high-ranking FSB officers was offered with their unquestioned approval.

Aside from shared investigations, training exchanges, and other attempts at building trust, Viktor must have had a sense of the operations directed at us by his FSB colleagues. And in the event of a pitch—if someone had picked up compromising information on the legat staff— Viktor would have been the perfect "good cop" complement to his part- ner's "bad cop." A potential bad cop might have been my counterpart in Washington, DC, Sergei, the FSB colonel in charge of the liaison office at the Russian Embassy.[4] Sergei had an interesting past, having been awarded the coveted Hero of the Soviet Union medal for bravery during the Soviet occupation of Afghanistan, the war the Soviets fought against CIA-backed mujahideen guerrilla fighters. More than once my Russian colleagues reminded me of the mujahideen's deadly use of US Stinger missiles, allegedly supplied by the CIA, to down Soviet helicopters. Those attacks resulted in the deaths of their fellow soldiers; not a small matter for the Russians, it was something they were unlikely to ever forget—and certainly not Sergei.

As the saying goes, "Countries don't have friends; countries have interests." And so Viktor and I were strange bedfellows—natural adver- saries who enjoyed our search for a common purpose, working in a world in which, had we let our guard down and become friends, our respective countrymen would have suspected us of betraying our coun- tries. Had I not gotten to know him, I would have thought of Viktor as the "other." But to an extent, I did get to know him, and without the invisible stone wall that defined our world, I would like to think we might have become lifelong friends, bound by debates over our different worldviews, founded on mutual respect. Had that been the case, Viktor would have remained my only connection to what has rapidly become a not-so-brave new (Russian) world that is alien and untethered, spinning deeper into the cosmos by the day. But when all was said and done, there was never any doubt that once I left Moscow, whatever camaraderie we had would quickly fade away. And so it did. But a photograph of this good man hangs in my home, a reminder of a friendship that might have been.

CHAPTER 15

Their Country, Their Rules

You Get to Go Home

EVERY CAREER HAS A SHELF LIFE, AND I COULD READ THE EXPIRATION date on mine: January 31, 2007. Like my predecessor before me (and in his words), I was "tired of the bear hug." I was tired of living with the demon at the door in a world governed by Moscow rules: unofficial guidelines for Americans working in Moscow who might be of intelligence value to the Russians.[1] Under Moscow rules we had to assume that "everyone was potentially under opposition control"[2] (rule no. 3), and of course, that assumption worked both ways: each of us had to assume that we, too, were under that hazy cloud of suspicion by our American colleagues. Moscow rule no. 4 warned that we were "never completely alone,"[3] and therefore, we had to watch what we did and said, knowing that wherever we went, someone was watching, and whatever we said, someone was listening. Boiled down to their essence, Moscow rules demanded that we adjust to a world in which we were always being scrutinized—examined for personal weakness and disloyalty—in a world where "Trust, but verify" was a test of loyalty, smiles concealed hidden agendas, and privacy was a distant memory. It was a murky world where people were not always who they said they were, where their intentions were not always what they claimed to be, and where trust had to be constantly reaffirmed. And to maintain that trust, we had to put privacy aside, remain transparent, and accept that our fellow Americans may now and then set a few traps to reassure themselves of our loyalty. After years on both ends of that microscope, I was tired and tired of being tired, looking forward to the day I could let go and indulge the sentiment behind survival rule no. 2: "Their country, their rules; you get to go home."

Moscow embassy culture was such that, to catch Americans in a compromising position, the Russians watched our every move. But they weren't alone. The US government also tracked us in an ongoing attempt to counter those Russian efforts. Like the world of the Las Vegas characters in the movie *Casino*, "The dealers are watching the players. The box men are watching the dealers. The floor men are watching the box men. The pit bosses are watching the floor men. The shift bosses are watching the pit bosses . . . and the eye in the sky is watching us all."[4] In the case of any personal contacts with non-US citizens, we had to report identifying details and explanations to both FBIHQ and the RSO. And although I socialized with CIA intelligence officers on a regular basis, I assumed they were scrutinizing me as well, with one eye on the nature of my Russian contacts, activities, and interests.

Given the Moscow rules assumption that everyone was under opposition control, safeguards designed to counter that possibility were a part of our daily lives. In my case, I sometimes found myself on the receiving end of unsolicited, highly sensitive information that I had absolutely no need to know. If accurate, that information would have been of significant value to the Russians. Why? I will never know for sure, but the answer to that question has haunted me for years. One obvious possibility is that I was being set up, not by the Russians but by my FBI colleagues in Washington, DC, that I was given disinformation: singular bits of manufactured US-intelligence fictions designed as a test to determine if that information would reach the Russians. If there were indications that this information did reach the Russians, I would then have been suspected of being the source—a Russian mole within the FBI's inner sanctum. On the other hand, if there were no indications that the information had leaked, there would be no basis on which to believe I had become the next Robert Hanssen. Of course, I will never know why anyone felt the need to share information I should never have been told, and yes, it could have simply been a case of my paranoia. But that's the point. That's the foggy world of life in Moscow, where it is sometimes difficult to figure out what is real and what is an illusion.

Having made the decision to retire, I submitted my retirement papers to FBIHQ, fully expecting to be polygraphed prior to my departure. To me, that was a logical expectation, given the information at my fingertips and my years working in the former Soviet Union, especially in Moscow, where I'd been in regular contact with the FSB. To my surprise, there were no plans to do so, and therefore, even as uncomfortable as polygraphs can be under the best of circumstances, I requested a polygraph to preempt any questions down the road. In short, I wanted to leave both Moscow and the FBI with a clean slate, with no lingering concerns as to any improper sharing of information with the Russians.

At my request, I was polygraphed at FBIHQ soon after submitting my retirement papers. As expected, the polygrapher's principal focus was whether I had ever knowingly mishandled classified information or shared such information with the Russians—acts that would have extended well beyond gross violations of FBI policy into egregious violations of federal law. Not a problem. But to my great surprise, the polygraph didn't end there, as the polygrapher threw me an unanticipated curveball: "Are there any FBI personnel who have any derogatory information about you?" And what was my response to that landmine-laden question? "Over what period of time?" I'm sure the polygrapher sensed a bit of discomfort as he explained, "Over your entire career, since you were sworn in." I was dumbfounded but, truth be told, slightly amused as I mentally scanned the previous twenty-two years and imagined the reactions of my closest agent friends from years gone by, had they been given the chance to watch me squirm and tap dance around that tricky question.

Amusement on the part of my oldest agent friends would have stemmed from our shared experience during simpler but wilder times, long before any of us could have imagined an FBI agent passing deadly critical intelligence to the Russians or shielding a violent organized crime boss. It was a time when our dedication to a team effort was the sole yardstick by which we were measured as agents, long before anyone felt the need to break into ethnic, gender, or racially divided camps.

We were a family whose commitment to each other and the FBI was lifelong. And despite our personal flaws, we'd remained laser focused on the high-stakes mission we believed in so deeply. In those simpler times, the only way agents got into trouble was by failing to adhere to rigorous standards of behavior that had been around since the days of J. Edgar Hoover—boundaries defined by an internal code of personal conduct that required little bureaucratic vernacular and that boiled down to one simple admonition: "Never embarrass the Bureau!"

In response to the polygrapher's inquiry into my past, I offered to delve into my personal history and revisit times I may have hovered near the ghost of Mr. Hoover's bright line. But the polygrapher graciously spared us both what would have been an interesting trip down memory lane, and with a wave of his arms and a firm "No!" took it no further. When all was said and done, the polygrapher told me I passed the exam, although it seemed I may have experienced a bit of discomfort with that last question. Imagine that.

Following my polygraph, as I was preparing to put Moscow and the FBI behind me, thinking of how much the FBI had changed over two decades was just the first step in the break from what would soon be my past. The next steps focused on a flood of questions, not the least of which centered on how I might reinvent myself now that my deeply ingrained identity was about to be dismantled. But my more immediate question was, What had I accomplished in Moscow? And as I pondered that challenging question, I had a hard time shaking off another provocative Russian proverb: "A bad dancer always blames his balls for getting in the way" (Плохому танцору яйца всегда мешают).

Figuring out what I had accomplished in Moscow was complicated, given that my work in the former Soviet Union was nothing like the early days of my stateside career, when our accomplishments were splashed on the front pages of newspapers, the rescue of innocent victims was a clear win, and success was measured in convictions of criminal defendants and lengthy prison sentences. Legat life was different. Success was harder to measure, especially without those tangible, gold-standard results that my predecessors had achieved. Those accomplishments began in the mid-1990s, when the first legat and his partner built the Moscow office from the ground up, faced with the monumental task of earning the trust of a longtime adversary and turning that hard-earned trust into the arrest of notorious organized crime figures both in the US and Russia. Those celebrated, early achievements laid the foundation for my more recent predecessors, who coordinated high-profile investigations such as that which led to the arrest of an international arms smuggler who was determined to help bring down US civilian aircraft. As I left Moscow, I counted among my achievements a strengthening of the bridge between the FBI and FSB that would allow for future accomplishments, nurturing cases that my ALAT partners would one day bring to fruition and, through cross-training with HRT, prompting the FSB Alpha Team to approach crisis situations with a more professional, hostage-friendly mindset. But given all the changes in Russia since my retirement, most of what I once proudly thought of as my professional achievements have proven to have had an expiration date of their own.

Amid those questions, I thought of all I would miss about Moscow and the FBI. I would miss the fabric of embassy life, where we interacted with counterparts from all over the world who were part of an ongoing global narrative. I would miss taking part in country team meetings, where experts in their specialized fields shared their insights into events as they were happening, and where I got a glimpse of Russia through the eyes of Ambassador William Burns—the future director of the CIA. Those were opportunities of a lifetime. I would also miss the professionalism of the US servicemen and women, who had played so many critical roles in the US Embassy. High on that list were the Marine Security Guards—everyone's friends, who watched out for us and regularly hosted parties at their embassy living quarters, where there was always plenty to eat, plenty of laughs, and plenty of stories. And in some respects, I would miss the challenge, and yes, the high-stakes "game" that went along with working with my Russian counterparts.

But most of all, I would miss the sense of adventure that goes with living and working in another culture, watching a part of history unfold as Russia dabbled in democracy and went on to reassemble its Soviet past. On another level, I knew I would miss the privileges that had been part of my everyday life: my diplomatic passport—a lifeline to sanity that insulated me from police corruption and a weaponized Russian judicial system, as well as my FBI credentials, which, for twenty-two years, symbolized who I was to my core, with side benefits that included bypassing airport security, given my authority to carry a weapon on all domestic flights. Now, in the weeks leading to my retirement, having turned in my FBI credentials, I was humbled after being chastised by TSA for carrying toothpaste in my briefcase—a wake-up call if there ever was one, signaling the many adjustments I would soon be making to my new post-FBI life.[5]

In a strange way, I knew I would miss the never-ending odysseys of life in Russia. Not the least of those were the widespread, absurd conspiracy theories being peddled by Russian leaders, nurtured by the media, and accepted by people who, for some mysterious reason, seemed capable of believing anything: how bird flu then spreading in Russia stemmed from an American conspiracy to disrupt Russia's economic recovery, as well as the crazy tales of adopted Russian babies, whose organs were supposedly being sold for profit by their new American adoptive parents. Clearly, those who fell for that insanity never flew the Delta flights from Moscow to JFK, which were packed with young American couples celebrating the happiest days of their lives as they tenderly cradled their newly adopted Russian children, full of love and hope for the future. And yet so many Russians succumbed to the power of ridiculous rumors voiced by the media and nourished by those in power, convinced of the truth of those outrageous absurdities—a situation that eventually contributed to a Russian government ban on adoption of Russian children by Americans. And in those days, I was naïve enough to believe that such insanely destructive conspiracy theories were unique to Russians.

My last days as an FBI agent proved to be far different than what I would have experienced had I retired from an office in the US, where gatherings tended toward bittersweet celebrations centered on shared stories and heartfelt goodbyes to people the retirees had known for years. Those functions generally consisted of an unlikely assortment of unique personalities drawn from a wide range of political beliefs and cultural backgrounds who somehow came together to share in a common cause. Those gatherings were an opportunity to revel in recognition of career accomplishments and wince at painful reminders of the least flattering moments of one's career—one last chance for the sharks to draw blood along with a few laughs. But at their core, they were an emotional good-bye to a collection of colorful characters the retiree had grown to love as members of his or her extended family—a family in which occasional yet passionate disagreements were almost always tempered by mutual respect, a shared sense of purpose, and lifelong, unbreakable bonds.

Retiring out of Moscow was a vastly different experience. Although most of my State Department coworkers knew me, no one knew me well. And although they were always good to me, they simply weren't the people I had grown with over the course of my career. But they offered a sincere gesture of respect by hosting a well-attended party at the embassy's Liberty Bar on the evening before my departure. For that I was extremely grateful. Among the honored guests were the two FBI ALATs whose partnership I had come to deeply appreciate during my Moscow assignment. Also present was the US Marine Security Guard master sergeant, who presented me with a flag that had flown over the embassy upon the death of former president Gerald Ford. And there was the new US military attaché who, having arrived in Moscow on my last day, introduced himself and graciously thanked me for my service. That deeply appreciated sentiment got my wheels turning. Thanks for my service? In fact, my entire career had been an e-ride: a nonstop series of adventures, friendships, triumphs, painful defeats, indelible memories, a sense of purpose, and just plain fun. And someone was *thanking* me for that? No, I should be thanking every person who had given me the opportunity to live the career of a lifetime.

As for the Russians, FSB chairman Nikolai Patrushev recognized my retirement with a small farewell gift presented to me at an annual FSB-hosted gathering of intelligence officials. That same evening I was interviewed on Moscow television about my work with the FSB, an event arranged by FSB officials and cautiously preapproved by the US Embassy Public Affairs officer. From FBI friends in the US and across the globe, I received heartfelt emails that brought back two decades of shared memories. As for FBIHQ, I received an email congratulating me on my retirement.

As I reflected on my retirement, I concluded that I had seen the last, best ten years of the FBI. But in truth, that impression is undoubtedly shared by every retiree from every generation of FBI agents—past, present, and future—going back to my highly regarded mentors who served under the man most reverently still referred to as Mr. Hoover. Over time retirees from every generation long for the bygone days when the FBI functioned as it did during their careers. What is difficult to grasp is that times change, our culture changes, the nature of the threat changes, and the FBI we knew and loved changes. But regardless of those differences, what all generations of FBI personnel have in common is the call to respond to what our culture sees as the most immediate and dangerous threats. In my generation those dangers included terrorism (domestic and international), violent crime, violations of civil rights, white supremacists, organized crime, cyber crime, drugs, public corruption, crimes against children, white collar fraud, the Soviets, China, and later, the Russians. Like my FBI colleagues, I took pride in responding to those threats professionally, within the ironclad boundaries of the Constitution. Because when all is said and done, no matter how much the times change, loyalty to the Constitution, an unbiased commitment to enforcing federal law, and playing by the hard and fast rules those documents demand are the unwavering principles that guide FBI agents—not personalities, not political idols, or how any one person, however powerful or persuasive, defines "enemies of the people."

As I looked back, I came to appreciate the unique opportunities that working Russian organized crime, years of interactions with police officers at the International Law Enforcement Academy, and living/working in the former Soviet Union had afforded me. Those experiences offered a rare glimpse into the dynamics that were shaping Russian life and left me with valuable insights into the people and country that played an outsized role in my youth. With that front-row seat came an insider's view of the changes taking place on the ground in Russia, including the glaring contrast between Moscow in 1998 and Moscow in 2007, a period when Russia began its descent on a slippery slope from a budding democracy to a familiar style of autocratic leadership. And as it continues down that slope, Russia is once again throwing down the Cold War gauntlet at the feet of American democratic values and institutions. Only this time, those same values and institutions appear to be under threat, not just from external forces, but from internal forces as well.

CHAPTER 16

Oh Say, Can You (Still) See . . .

WHAT APPEARED TO BE THE BEGINNING OF THE END OF THE COLD WAR
was an event most of my generation will remember as vividly as we recall
the shock of the Cuban Missile Crisis. It was that day in November
1989 when Western liberal democracy won the battle of ideas over autocracy and communism. It was the moment we breathed a collective sigh of
relief as we watched families separated by years of fear and Soviet oppression tearfully reunite in the streets of Berlin. And although President
George H. W. Bush presided over that historic moment, to my mind,
it was Ronald Reagan who, backed up and empowered by our collective
faith in democracy, our shared trust in our system of government, and
the strength of our European alliances, had steered a clear path toward
the end of the Cold War by resolutely asserting American leadership and
supporting those dying in the fight against Soviet aggression. He did so
not just in words but by going eyeball-to-eyeball with Soviet leadership,
by flexing American military, economic and scientific muscle through the
Strategic Defense Initiative, through his firm support of the solidarity
movement in Poland, and his skill in communicating directly with Soviet
citizens on Soviet media. That was a happy ending for us and our allies,
including the extremists among us who were known for the battle cry
"Better dead than Red" and who believed that death was preferable to
living under Soviet communism.

I am certainly no expert on war, and to be clear, I never served in
the military. But from the point of view of one who has spent much of
his life with the Cold War, the Soviet Union, and Russia on his mind,

there is more than one way to define "winning" a war. One might be a country's ability to force its adversary to its knees with an unambiguous, ceremonial surrender. That assumes, of course, that there are adversaries on both sides still standing—an assumption that was challenged by the Cold War concept of mutually assured destruction (MAD), a theoretical deterrent to nuclear war built on the premise that no country would be insane enough to initiate an attack that would assuredly result in its own total destruction. And with fresh memories of the unimaginable horrors suffered by hundreds of thousands of Japanese men, women, and children in Hiroshima and Nagasaki in the collective mind, mutually assured destruction came with a foreboding sense of the possible.

For many of us, the beauty in the way the Cold War ended was its lack of a direct confrontation and violent conclusion: no ballistic missiles fired across continents, no mass casualties or body bags on European battlefields, and no irradiated cities leveled to the ground. It was a victory of ideologies and values: a thriving Western liberal democracy based on capitalism versus a broken autocracy based on communism. It was a victory embodied in the collapse of the Soviet Union and in Russia's early attempts to emulate the West by building a democratic, capitalist society. To be sure, I miss the days following the end of the Cold War, when there was a palpable but brief sense of a common purpose, made evident to me personally as my coworkers and I engaged with our Russian colleagues toward common goals, especially in the late 1990s. In hindsight, and at the risk of sounding melodramatic, the 1990s now remind me of the Christmas truces of World War I, when, in December 1914, after years of animosity between countries and months of hopeless despair and destruction on the western front, soldiers from each side briefly came out of their trenches to exchange food, souvenirs, and a shared sense of compassion. In that magical moment, deadly adversaries overcame a primordial, tribal urge to destroy the "other" to feed another powerful urge: the need to share a common humanity.

But now that we are back in our trenches, we take our eyes off Russia at our peril. In hindsight, that Putin has successfully altered the democratic trajectory of the 1990s by returning Russia to Soviet-style government control should surprise no one. Nor should it surprise us that he has recreated an atmosphere intolerant of dissent, epitomized by his 2022 declaration that all "true (Russian) patriots" support the "special military operation" in Ukraine and that those who do not are "scum and traitors."[1] But what should surprise us is that, as Putin is rebuilding Russia in his image, America is in danger of allowing the very values, principles, and institutions that were the hallmarks of our Cold War victory to weaken. And as this transformation takes place, Putin, the leader of a once-defeated system, is taking delight in the belief that his calculated efforts to sow internal discord, mistrust, and confusion in the United States have abetted this erosion, giving him cover to retroactively claim a Cold War victory without firing a shot and without the mutually assured destruction that would have resulted from nuclear war.

We see the manifestations of internal discord, mistrust, and confusion when a free society's answers to the Russian *siloviki*—US law enforcement, prosecutors, the intelligence community, and the military—are pressured by political leaders to make an absurd, Soviet-style choice: offer blind loyalty to an individual in lieu of their oath to the Constitution or be accused of treason. Or when the most vulnerable US citizens are disenfranchised, the result of concerted efforts to restrict their right to vote. And we see seeds of destruction when, to hold government's feet to the fire, journalists who challenge our political leaders based on debatable yet reasonable assertions of fact are vilified by those using Stalin's deadly vicious phrase "enemies of the people"—a hop, skip, and a jump from unsupported claims of spreading "fake news," an obscene term that should make our skin crawl.

We should sense danger when our most basic democratic principles are challenged from within—the right to have one's vote count without having to defend against unsupported claims of fraud made by armchair experts on the Constitution who ignore fair-minded decisions of legitimate Constitutional experts in federal and state courts; when rioters infected by the politics of polarization take a chainsaw to democracy through attacks on our legislature as it attempts to fulfill its sacred Constitutional duties; and when political leaders pressure prosecutors to target political enemies, forgetting that prosecutors are obligated to bring criminal charges based only on the law, facts and evidence provable in court, and not on feel-good assertions made during rousing speeches to their followers. America's defining ideals—your vote is your voice, the peaceful transfer of power, freedom of the press, the rule of law, an independent judiciary, all men (and women) are created equal—are not just feel-good phrases. And our institutions—the courts, the intelligence community, the military, the Department of Justice, the Department of State, and the FBI—are not at the disposal of any one individual. These concepts and institutions were the backbone of the democracy that made us strong enough to claim a moral victory without firing a shot. Undermining US democracy comes straight out of the Vladimir Putin playbook, with its dedicated chapter on feeding internal polarization by tapping into anger and division and playing those with different view-points against each other. Those chessboard moves beg the following question: Can Soviet-style calls for "self-purification" and "citizen infor-mants" be far away?

Many on both sides of this uncivil, internal American debate are using the same deflections that were typical of my FSB colleagues: the outward-directed "whataboutisms" that opposing sides use to dodge self-examination and accountability. For those in the FSB, these were natural responses from adherents to a governing philosophy that had, for decades, followed the unofficial motto "Logic is the enemy, and truth is a menace." It was a way of thinking that is anathema to intellectual honesty—the willingness to self-reflect without regard to what we wish to be true. As one who has fallen into that trap many times, I believe that if we forget how to look in the mirror, we forget who we are. And if we succumb to that way of responding to challenges, we end up dismissing truths simply because they fly in the face of our worldview—we leave ourselves open to baseless, *Alice in Wonderland*-type conspiracy theories, and we risk blindly accepting the word of mortal men or women as hav-ing come from the burning bush. In so doing, we leave ourselves vulner-able to the words of Max von Sydow's character in *The Exorcist*, Father Merrin, who warned that his adversary will "lie to confuse us, but he will also mix lies with the truth to attack us. His attack is psychological. And powerful."[2]

In the early days of my Russian adventure, I was caught off guard by a question posed to me by a former Muscovite: How would I define America? My less-than-scholarly response went something like this: America is a country that, despite its flaws, is built on enduring governing principles and a moral compass that have always inspired us to seek out and try to do the right thing. I believed that then, and I believe it now. But amid our painful struggle to figure out a modern-day definition of the right thing, we have descended into an uncivil wrestling match that has muddled our daily dialogue.

As we grapple in the mud, a reincarnated Soviet Union is using its ever-fading facade of democracy and an ever-shrinking measure of credibility to point a finger at our democracy's failings. As for the ghosts of Soviet leaders past, I imagine them taking satisfaction in the conclusion that, when push came to shove, there was no need for the bomb. Why threaten violence when you can sit back and let your enemy slowly tear itself apart? Put another way, who needs nukes when your adversary is paralyzed by internal feuds, which are further inflamed by those who allow Soviet-style language and ideas to infect the conversation? During the Cold War, the threat was external and there for all to see. Today? The threat is more insidious as it creeps up slowly from within and gradually erodes our values and codes of civil conduct. And if the threat continues unabated, we will find ourselves assuming our Cold War posture once again, with one eye on that dormant bomb shelter and the other eye on each other. And that's not good.

Like in the heady days following the collapse of the Soviet Union, how to define America and how we define doing "the right thing" are once again questions that demand an answer from all of us with a stake in the future. That includes those of us of a certain age who grew up under threat of nuclear war, who benefitted from our political leaders' unflinching stand against autocracy and that huge democratic stone our parents rolled uphill, and who are now responsible for passing on a dignified concept of America to our heirs. How we define America is certainly of interest not only to our heirs but to immigrants from the former Soviet Union, who, having been hoodwinked as children into believing that communism was the promised land, now have a reason for cynicism as we struggle with our once agreed-upon democratic ideals. And the answer is equally important to those living in aspiring democracies that have traditionally held America up as a role model.

But to all, I would add a follow-up question: Do we really want America's path to the "right thing" to be guided by Soviet signposts that are misdirecting and contaminating our conversation and, in some cases, are mistaken for acceptable paths to political success? Or should Soviet-style language and tactics be called out for what they are—part of a dangerous political strategy that, in the short term, threatens to reshape and derail our values, our institutions, and our alliances and, in the long run, threatens to reshape who we will become? And without those dead-end detours in the conversation, it just might be possible to do a better job of listening to the "other" in our own backyard, each of whom has his or her own story to tell.

Notes

Chapter 1

1. Operation Greylord was a groundbreaking FBI undercover case that successfully targeted rampant bribery and corruption within several branches of the Circuit Court of Cook County; the events were dramatically depicted in a fascinating book of the same name by former undercover agent Terrence Hake.

Chapter 2

1. "How the Bear Became the Symbol of Russia," *Russia Beyond*, June 10, 2019, Ekaterina Sinelschikova.

2. Prior to its collapse in 1991, the Soviet Union strictly controlled travel to and from its borders. Jewish Soviets were the first to receive permission to emigrate in significant numbers, starting in the 1970s.

3. In retrospect those early successes at finding cracks in US government programs would portend future Russian-based ransomware attacks that began plaguing US government agencies and businesses in 2021.

4. "Bank of New York Settles Protracted Russian Lawsuit," *New York Times*, September 16, 2009, Andrew Kramer.

5. The term *Russian organized crime* is more accurately known as Russian-*speaking* organized crime or *Eurasian* organized crime to include criminals from all former Soviet republics.

6. Common Russian expressions will be presented in both English and Russian throughout the book.

7. "Communist Party of the Soviet Union," factsanddetails.com.

8. Yeltsin's Speech, August 19, 1991, as translated by the US State Departmen.

9. "The Looting of Russia," *US New and World Report*, August 3, 1998, David Kaplan and Christian Caryl.

10. The legal attaché (legat) is the head of the relevant overseas FBI post. He or she answers to two bosses: FBI Headquarters (FBIHQ) and the US ambassador. In the early 2000s, the FBI had legats and assistant legats in over fifty countries.

11. Lazarenko's theft from the government of Ukraine was a prime example of the term *kleptocracy*, a "government by those who seek status and personal gain at the expense of

the governed." The term gained notoriety following the breakup of the Soviet Union. www.merriam-webster.com/dictionary.

12. This quote was the punchline to a joke circulating in the San Francisco Russian-speaking community in the late 1990s. It was a joke I overheard at a party among Russian friends.

13. "Moscow Heating Pipes Create Lethal Traps," *Los Angeles Times*, April, 7, 1998, Richard Paddock.

14. The movie *The Irony of Fate* is the story of an intoxicated Muscovite who is mistakenly put on a plane to Leningrad by his equally intoxicated friends. There he uses his key to access an apartment that looks just like his, with the same street address and furniture. In a rare case of a Russian happy ending, the tenant in his Leningrad look-alike apartment is a beautiful woman with whom he falls in love.

CHAPTER 3

1. In September 1991, in a huge blow to veteran KGB officers, the new head of the KGB turned over blueprints of the locations of those listening devices to the US ambassador in Russia.

2. "Cleaning the Bug House," *Air and Space Forces Magazine*, September 1, 2012, Peter Grier, https://www.airandspaceforces.com/article/0912embassy/.

3. "Senate Report Faults CIA for Ineptitude in Spy Case," *New York Times*, November 2, 1994, Tim Weiner.

CHAPTER 4

1. There is a grain of truth to the stereotypes associated with Soviet dental care, as I learned from former Soviets and their experience with Soviet dentists. These are the stuff of childhood nightmares that most who grew up during Soviet times can relate to.

2. "US Marine Attacked by Neo-Nazis in Moscow," *Los Angeles Times*, May 4, 1998, Richard C. Paddock.

3. Yakov Smirnoff was well-known Russian comedian who became popular in the US in the 1970s-1980s. "What a country" was the tag line he attached to most of his comedy routines.

4. I generally toasted to my preference for pointing shot glasses at each rather than missiles.

CHAPTER 6

1. Fourteen years later, Dutbayev would land in a Kazakh prison, convicted of leaking state secrets and abuse of office.

2. Russia still uses the Baikonur Cosmodrome for launches into space, having secured a lease from Kazakhstan until 2050.

3. "Arrest Warrant for Kazakh Billionaire Accused of One of World's Biggest Frauds," *The Guardian*, February 16, 2012, Rupert Neate.

4. "Oil, Cash and Corruption," *New York Times*, November 5, 2006, Ron Stodghill.

5. "Former Kazakh National Security Chief Imprisoned," *Radio Free Europe/Radio Liberty*, September 11, 2017, RFE/RL's Kazakh Service.

6. Foreign service nationals are locally employed, non-American embassy staff who provide support services to and are paid by the US government.

7. Attacks on a US Embassy fall under US terrorism law, title 18, chapter 113B, section 2332.

8. The PGO bomber's original plan may have been to attack the nearby British Embassy.

9. "Suicide Bomb Kills Two," *Associated Press*, updated September 27, 2019, Bert Herman.

10. From the song "Camp Granada" by Allen Sherman.

CHAPTER 7

1. Poem by Boris Zakhoder.

2. "A Lesson in Russian Strategic Deception," *Slate*, November 3, 2017, John Sipher.

3. Disinformation, along with deception, sabotage, and propaganda, is one category of KGB counterintelligence offensives collectively known as *active measures*.

4. *Spy Handler, Memoir of a KGB Officer*, Viktor Cherkashin and Gregory Feifer, 2005, Basic Books.

5. *A Review of the FBI's Performance in Deterring, Detecting, and Investigating the Espionage Activities of Robert Philip Hanssen*, 2003, US Department of Justice, Office of Inspector General, Glenn Fine.

6. At the time of this writing, Patrushev still holds a position of significant power in Russia as secretary of the Security Council of the Russian Federation, a position he has held since 2008.

7. This was a quote of a senior FBI Counterintelligence official as he and I spoke privately outside the office of Director Mueller at FBI Headquarters in the minutes leading to the meeting between Director Mueller and FSB Chairman Patrushev.

8. Yuri Vladimirovich Andropov was the head of the KGB from 1967 to 1982. In 1982 he replaced Leonid Brezhnev as general secretary of the Communist Party and, therefore, leader of the Soviet Union.

9. In 2011, four years after my departure from Moscow, a new law enforcement investigative agency was created. Known as the investigative committee, it is sometimes referred to as the Russian FBI. During my years in Moscow, the FSB's mission more directly mirrored that of the FBI.

10. Years later, one of the two ALATs assigned to my office would be promoted to the position of legat in Moscow in a far more hostile environment. At that time tensions between the US and Russia were high, exemplified by a physical attack by an FSB embassy guard on a US diplomat in 2016.

11. In 2021 President Biden appointed Ambassador Burns director of the CIA.

12. In addition to being responsible for the security of the embassy, the RSO's office is also responsible for the protection of the US ambassador.

13. United States v. Hemant Lakhani, Appellant, 480 F.3d 171 (3rd Cir. 2007).

CHAPTER 8

1. Charles Colson was Special Counsel to President Richard Nixon from 1969-1970. The quote is taken from a plaque that was said to have hung in Colson's office. The quote is also cited in the movie, "All the President's Men" (1976).

CHAPTER 10

1. *The Main Enemy: The Inside Story of the CIA's Final Showdown with the KGB*, Milt Bearden and James Risen, 2004, Penguin Random House.

2. "The KGB Rises Again in Russia," *Los Angeles Times*, January 12, 2000, R. C. Paddock.

3. "Vladimir Putin Resurrects the KGB," *Politico*, September 16, 2016, Owen Matthews.

4. "Khrushchev's Secret Speech, 'On the Cult of Personality and Its Consequences,'" *Wilson Center Digital Archive*, February 25, 1956 (uploaded December 17, 2012), Nikita S. Khrushchev, https://digitalarchive.wilsoncenter.org/document/khrushchevs-secret -speech-cult-personality-and-its-consequences-delivered-twentieth-party.

5. In contrast to the KGB's pledge of loyalty to an ideology and political party, FBI agents pledge an oath to the US Constitution. In a system based on rule of law and checks and balances, agents answer not only to superiors within the executive branch but are subject to oversight by Congress and judicial rulings in federal courts.

6. "Soviet Paper Says KGB Helped Oust Khrushchev," *Washington Post*, September 15, 1988, Michael Dobbs.

7. *The Man Without a Face - The Unlikely Rise of Vladimir Putin*, Masha Gessen, Riverhead Books, 2012.

8. "Articles 70 and 27" from *A Chronicle of Current Events-For Human Rights and Freedom of Expression in the USSR*

9. In the museum hung a photo of my FSB counterpart in Washington, DC, who was awarded the Hero of the Soviet Union medal for acts during the Soviet occupation in Afghanistan.

10. "Andropov's KGB: Pervasive Force in Soviet," New York Times, 11/16/82, Richard Bernstein.

11. "Kremlin Counts on Informers to Keep Soviet Society in Line," *Christian Science Monitor*, July 5, 1983, Ted Nemko.

12. "Yeltsin Immunity Upheld by Duma Vote," *Washington Post*, March 30, 2000, David Hoffman.

13. "Dmitry Medvedev's Government Steps Down," *Kommersant*, January 15, 2020.

14. "Russian Patriarch Calls Putin Era, 'Miracle of God'" *Reuters*, 2/8/2012, Gleb Bryanski

CHAPTER 11

1. From the website of the Society for Professional Journalists (spj.org), SPJ Code of Ethics.

2. From a Russian-language article, "Эху Москвы исполнилось 25 лет", *Interfax*, 8/22/2015.

3. "The Kremlin Is Killing Echo of Moscow, Russia's Last Independent Radio Station," *The Daily Beast*, November 7, 2014, Anna Nemtsova.

4. "Last Vestiges of Russia's Free Press Fall Under Kremlin Pressure," *New York Times*, March 3, 2022, Anton Troianovski and Valeriya Safronova.

5. In 2021 Dmitry Muratov was awarded the Nobel Peace Prize. In June 2022 he took a bold and selfless stand by donating $103.5 million in proceeds from the sale of his Nobel Prize medal to UNICEF, in support of Ukrainian child refugees.

6. "Russia's Novaya Gazeta Cuts Ukraine War Reporting under Censorship," *Reuters*, March 4, 2022, Mark Trevelyan.

7. "Tales from Hoffman," *Index on Censorship* 37, no. 1 (October 2008).

8. "Kremlin Accused of Dirty Tactics to Take Over Media," ABC.net, September 20, 2000, Irris Makler.

9. *The Man without a Face: The Unlikely Rise of Vladimir Putin*, Masha Gessen, 2012, Riverhead Books.

10. Up until its expulsion in 2022, the Russian Federation was a member of the Council of Europe and a party to the European Convention on Human Rights. As such, Russia was subject to rulings by the European Court of Human Rights. For more information on Litvinenko, see "Russia Responsible for Litvinenko Death Court Rules," *The Guardian*, September 21, 2021, Haroon Siddique and Andrew Roth.

11. "Russian TV Station Proclaims 'No To War,' Plays 'Swan Lake' Before Going Dark", *Huffpost*, 3/3/2022, Hilary Hansen.

12. "TV Rain, Russia's Last Independent TV Channel, Airs Symbolic Protest on Final Broadcast," *Deadline*, March 3, 2022, Tom Tapp.

13. "'The Point is to Scare Viewers'-TV Rain Editor-in-Chief Tikhon Dzyadko Speaks to Meduza About Joining the Ranks of Russia's 'Undesirable' Organizations'", *Meduza*, 7/28/2023.

14. "Russia Labels Independent Broadcaster Dozhd 'Undesirable,'" *The Moscow Times*, July 25, 2023.

15. "Meet Dimitry Kiselyov, Putin's New Shock Jock", *The Daily Beast*, 7/11/2017, James Kirchick.

16. "Revoltingly Foul-Russian TV Makes Final Push to Discredit US Election," *Radio Liberty*, November 7, 2016, Tom Balmforth.

17. "Meet Dimitry Kiselyov, Putin's New Shock Jock", *The Daily Beast*, 7/11/2017, James Kirchick.

18. "Vladimir Putin, Conservative Icon," *The Atlantic*, December 20, 2013, Brian Whitmore.

19. "The Grand Theory Driving Putin to War," *New York Times*, March 22, 2022, Jane Burbank.

20. "The Ukraine War Divides the Orthodox Faithful," *New York Times*, April 18, 2022, Neil MacFarquhar and Sophia Kishkovsky; "Putin Hands Over Historic Icon to Church," *The Moscow Times*, May 16, 2023.

21. "Meet Dmitri Kiselyov, Putin's New Shock Jock," *Daily Beast*, July 11, 2017, James Kirchick.

22. "Russian Media Fights for Survival under Putin," *Voice of America*, July 19, 2020, Pete Cobus, Anna Plotnikova, and Danila Galperovich.

23. "Joseph Stalin in His Own Words," *Foundation for Economic Education*, 3/8/2023.

24. "Berezovsky, Putin, and an Absence of Respect," *The Moscow Times*, March 23, 2013, Alexander Bratersky.

25. "Mikhail Khodorkovsky on Life after Prison and Russia after Putin," *The Guardian*, February 26, 2014, Shaun Walker.

26. "Murder Charges Filed against Previously Imprisoned Russian Oligarch," *New York Times*, December 11, 2015, Ivan Nechepurenko.

27. "Russia: Corruption Scandal Could Shake Kremlin," *Radio Free Europe / Radio Liberty*, September 26, 2006, Victor Yasmann.

28. In November 2022 a Dutch court sentenced two Russians and a Ukrainian to life in prison in absentia for their role in the downing of flight 17.

29. "Russia Lost 220 Troops in Ukraine," *BBC News*, May 12, 2015.

30. "Alexei Navalny: Russia's Jailed Vociferous Putin Critic," *BBC*, 8/4/2023.

31. *The Gulag Archipelago, 1918–1956: An Experiment in Literary Investigation*, Aleksander Solzhenitsyn, 1997, Basic Books.

32. "FSB Team of Chemical Weapon Experts Implicated in Alexei Navalny Novichok Poisoning," *Bellingcat*, December 14, 2020.

33. "Who is Opposition Activist Vladimir Kara-Murza?" *The Moscow Times*, 5/11/2023, by *Novaya Gazeta-Europe*.

34. "Russia Opens a Criminal Case Accusing a Pro-Democracy Activist of Spreading 'False Information' about the War," *New York Times*, April 22, 2022, Anton Troianovski.

35. "How Marina Ovsyannikova Became Russia's Most Visible Anti-War Protester," *The Wall Street Journal*, 3/17/2022, Evan Gershkovich.

36. "The Mysterious Case of Marina O." *Politico*, 5/1/2022, Zoya Shevtalovich.

37. "They're Lying to You: Russian TV Employee Interrupts News Broadcast," *The Guardian*, March 14, 2022, Pjotr Sauer.

38. "Russia Detains a Former State Television Journalist Who Protested over the War," *New York Times*, August 10, 2022, Ivan Nechepurenko.

39. Song by Lin-Manuel Miranda.

40. "Moscow Theater Siege: Questions Remain Unanswered," *BBC*, October 24, 2012, Artem Krechetnikov.

41. "Flamethrowers Used at Beslan Siege," *The Independent*, October 24, 2004, Andrew Osborn.

42. "A Reversal over Beslan Only Fuels Speculation," *Moscow Times*, July 21, 2005.

43. "Beslan Rescue Lacked Direction Says Ex-FSB Head," *Radio Free Europe / Radio Liberty*, December 16, 2015.

44. "Tanks That Fired in Beslan Were under FSB Command," *The Jamestown Foundation*, November 23, 2015.

45. "Aching to Know," *Los Angeles Times*, August 27, 2005, Kim Murphy.

46. "Twilight of the Idols," Friedrich Nietzsche (1888).

CHAPTER 12

1. A Russian quote, sometimes attributed to Josef Stalin.

2. "Daley Family Collections: About Richard J. Daley," *University of Illinois Library*, updated June 7, 2023, https://researchguides.uic.edu/DaleyFamily/RJDbio.

3. The Chicago machine's power to hire and fire patronage workers based solely on political loyalty continued into the early 1980s, at which time a judicial ruling in a civil lawsuit severely limited that practice. That ruling immediately pumped the brakes on Chicago-style politics as had been practiced under Daley.

4. *Don't Make No Waves . . . Don't Back No Losers*, Milton L. Rakove, 1975, Indiana University Press.

5. Having said this, I found that in the three years I worked as an assistant precinct captain, no one in my precinct was ever discouraged from registering to vote or from voting. Nor, history aside, did I ever hear of anyone from the Democratic Party attempting to create votes out of thin air or cemeteries.

6. *"Were There Any Elections in the USSR?" Russia Beyond, 11/20/20, Nikolay Shevchenko.*

7. "Russia Tightens Legislation on 'Foreign Agents,'" *Deutsche Welle*, June 29, 2022.

8. "Russian Justice Ministry Expands 'Foreign Agents' List to Include Navalny Foundation," *Radio Free Europe / Radio Liberty*, December 26, 2020.

9. "Russian Court Orders Prominent Human Rights Group to Shut," *New York Times*, December 28, 2021, Ivan Nechepurenko and Andrew E. Kramer.

10. Criminal Code of the Russian Federation, Article 213.

11. "President signed the law on 'landing,'" info@nplaw.ru.

12. "Russia Intensifies Censorship Campaign, Pressuring Tech Giants," *New York Times*, February 26, 2022, Adam Satariano.

13. "Russian Blocks Access to Facebook," *NPR*, 3/4/2022, Bobby Allyn, Alina Selyukh.

14. "Russia Fights Back in Information War with Jail Warning," *Reuters*, March 4, 2022, Guy Faulconbridge.

15. "Spurred by Putin, Russians Turn on One Another over the War," *New York Times*, April 9, 2022, Anton Troianovski.

16. "Aging Rebel: Vladimir Zhirinovsky Is Enjoying Another Moment," *Moscow Times*, September 2, 2016, Eva Hartog.

17. "Who Is Zhirinovsky? Mysteries Shroud Russian Nationalist," *Washington Post*, December 18, 1993, Lee Hockstader.

18. "Who Is Zhirinovsky?" Hockstader.

19. "The Best of Vladimir Zhirinovsky, the Clown Prince of Russian Politics," *Vice*, August 10, 2013, Diane Bruk.

20. "Zhirinovsky Promises Brutal Dictatorship if He Wins Russian Election," *Moscow Times*, March 1, 2018.

21. "Russian Ultranationalist Zhirinovsky Reportedly Hospitalized in Serious Condition with Covid," *Radio Free Europe / Radio Liberty*, February 9, 2022.

22. "Zhirinovsky Cult Grows. All Power to the Leader," *New York Times*, April 5, 1994, Celestine Bohlen.

CHAPTER 13

1. Once an FBI background check is completed, an investigative report is forwarded to the White House for use by the president and US senators to determine a judicial nominee's suitability. The FBI simply reports its findings and has no other role in deciding a nominee's suitability.

2. "Appointing the Judges: Procedures for Selection of Judges of the Russian Federation," *International Commission of Jurists Report*, 2014, https://www.icj.org/wp-content/uploads/2014/11/RUSSIA-Selecting-the-judges-Publications-Reports-2014-Eng.pdf.

3. "How Russian Courts Create Their Own Reality," *IMRussia*, March 31, 2021, Igor Slabykh.

4. Ironically, the site of the last courtroom to which I'd been assigned was once the home of Chicago's most famous amusement park (Riverview Park).

5. "Putin-Style Rule of Law and the Prospects for Change," *Daedalus*, Spring 2017, Maria Popova.

6. Having said that, who can foresee what internal challenges Putin has created for himself through his 2022 decision to invade Ukraine?

7. This is attributed to Spanish writer and philosopher George Santayana.

8. "Overview of the Judicial System of the Russian Federation," Supreme Court of the Russian Federation website, supct.ru.

9. "Russian Court Orders Prominent Human Rights Group to Shut," *New York Times*, December 28, 2021, Ivan Nechepurenko and Andrew E. Kramer.

10. "Russian Court Orders Prominent Human Rights Group to Shut," *New York Times*, 12/28/2021, Ivan Nechepurenko, Andrew E. Kramer.

11. "Russian Court Orders Prominent Human Rights Group to Shut," *New York Times*, 12/28/2021, Ivan Nechepurenko, Andrew E. Kramer.

12. "Press Release," *The Nobel Prize*, October 7, 2022, Oslo, https://www.nobelprize.org/prizes/peace/2022/press-release/.

13. "Pro-Kremlin Youth Group, Nashi, to Be Revamped," *Russia Beyond*, March 7, 2013, Alexei Bausin.

14. "Hacked Emails Allege Russian Youth Group Nashi Paying Bloggers," *The Guardian*, February 7, 2012, Miriam Elder.

15. "Nashi—Russia's Youth Countermovement," *Open Democracy*, August 30, 2007, Armine Ishkanian.

16. "Network—Son of Nashi New Youth Group Seeks to Woo Russia's Middle Class," *Radio Free Europe / Radio Liberty*, July 3, 2014, Tom Balmforth.

17. "A Kremlin Youth Movement Goes Rogue," *Moscow Times*, April 8, 2016, Eva Hartog.

18. "How the Kremlin Is Militarizing Russian Society," *New York Times*, December 21, 2021, Anton Troianovski, Ivan Nechepurenko, and Valerie Hopkins.

19. "Putin Aims to Shape a New Generation of Supporters through Schools," *New York Times*, July 16, 2022, Anton Troianovski.

20. These and other atrocities have given birth to a new word in Ukrainian: рашизм (pronounced "roshism"), a play on words linking the political philosophy behind Russia's invasion to "fascism."

21. From the book, "1984" by George Orwell (1949).

CHAPTER 14

1. This is not his real name.

2. One such instance involved a request by the FSB for FBI assistance in identifying the Iraqi terrorists responsible for the 2006 abduction and murder of five Russian diplomats in Baghdad.

3. "A Lump of Rock, a Sophisticated Spying Device, and an Embassy Left Red-Faced," *The Independent*, January 24, 2006, Kim Sengupta and Andrew Osborn.

4. This is not his real name.

CHAPTER 15

1. The ten Moscow rules are on display at the International Spy Museum in Washington, DC.

2. "Moscow Rules," International Spy Museum, Washington, DC, www.spymuseum.org.

3. "Moscow Rules," International Spy Museum, Washington, DC, www.spymuseum.org

4. From the movie, "Casino" (1995), Directed by Martin Scorsese, Written by Nicholas Pileggi, Martin Scorsese.

5. FBI agents typically turn in their credentials and badge just before their retirement so that they can be mounted on a plaque for presentation.

CHAPTER 16

1. "Putin Assails Russians Who Back the West, Signaling More Repression," *New York Times*, March 16, 2022, Anton Troianovski.

2. From the movie, "The Exorcist" (1973), Directed by William Friedkin, Written by William Peter Blatty.

INDEX

OSCE. *See* Organization for Security and Cooperation in Europe
Ovsyannikova, Maria, 137, 168

Party of Crooks and Thieves, 135
Patio Pasta restaurant, 17
Patriarch Kirill, 116, 129
Patrushev, Nikolai, 86–87, 125–26, 133, 187, 199n6
People's Commissariat for Internal Affairs, 110
perekhod, 35
perestroika, 11
PGO. *See* Prosecutor General's Office (Russia, Kazakhstan, Uzbekistan).
Politburo, 112
Politkovskaya, Anna, 122, 126, 128, 130
polonium 210, 127
pozhaluista stick, 64
Prague Spring Revolt of 1968, 111
Pravda, 120
President Hotel, Ashgabat, 80
privatization, 11, 15, 131
Prologue, 85, 199n2
punitive psychiatry, 113
Pushkin, Alexander, 22
Pushkin Square, 36
Pussy Riot, 155–56
Putinjugend, 172
Putin's Palace, 135
Putin, Vladimir
Vladimirovich: dissent, 122–37,

192, 200n7, 201nn17–18, 203n5, 204n1; election to office, 114–17, 145–46, 150–54, 200n7; FSB/KGB control, 87–88, 109–110, 115, 138–44, 199n3; judicial control, 160–167; legislative control, 154–60, 203n16; media control, 121–30, 201n16; special military operation-Ukraine, 120–23, 127–29, 135–38, 155, 157–59, 173–74, 190, 200n4, 201nn13, 14, 22, 202n12, 203n6; youth movements, 169–75

Rachmaninov, Sergei, 16, 19
Racketeer Influenced Corrupt Organization, 37
Radio Free Europe/Radio Liberty, 120, 130, 155, 198n5, 201nn11, 20, 31, 202nn8, 18, 203n13
Rahmon, Emomali, 76
Reagan, Ronald, 3, 178, 191
Red October, 170
Red Square: Kremlin Towers, 18; Kremlin Wall Necropolis, 17; Lenin's Tomb, 17; St. Basil's Cathedral, 17
Red Terror, 20, 110
Regional Security Officer. 66–67, 92, 105, 182
Return of the Names, 169
Rezident-Soviet Embassy, 85
RIA Novosti, 129
Rice, Condoleezza, 159